From Dream to Reality
Principles for Building a
Non-Profit Organization

by Jerry Nance, PhD

President/CEO
Teen Challenge International—Southeast Region

From Dream to Reality
Principles for Building a Non-Profit Organization

2nd Edition

ISBN 978-0-9817280-4-9

Cover Design: Timothy Dickens

Printed by Color House Graphics, Grand Rapids, MI USA

Published by
Jeryl Lynn Nance
15 W. 10th Street
Columbus, Georgia 31901

Special Thanks to...

I owe a debt of love to my patient and loving wife, Libby. She has been supportive in the whole process of developing Teen Challenge in Florida, Georgia, around the nation, the Caribbean, and around the world. She is my faithful friend, counselor and loyal companion.

I want to express my deep appreciation to my three children for being supportive of their dad's work. It has not always been easy with me being out of town, working late or in another country, but they have always been understanding and patient. Deneé, Kristi, and Dustin.

The board of directors and advisory board of Teen Challenge deserve much recognition and appreciation. Bob Manderscheid, Tom Benigas, Mark Jakelsky, John Baschieri, Rev. Terry Raburn, Rev. Don Price, Bobby Thompson, Ken Enlow, Jim Blanchard, Randy Valimont, Scott Lingerfelt, and Dave Weier have served endless hours assisting me with the vision for this ministry.

Thanks to Tommy and Jean Nance, my dad and mom, for all their support, their hundreds of hours of volunteering, prayers, and encouragement. Thanks to my in-laws, Rev. Paul and Lane Palser, who have worked on staff with us and have been so faithful to encourage and support my leadership.

A special thanks goes out to the staff of Teen Challenge of Florida/Georgia who have followed the dream God has given and have faithfully served. I couldn't begin to name them all, but the staff members are the ones who deserve the praise for the success of this ministry. These men and women have worked endless hours, sacrificed and served faithfully during many trying times. I believe I have the best staff of any Teen Challenge in the world.

And last but not least, I want to say thanks to the donors who have made the dreams and visions of Teen Challenge a reality. Thanks to all of you who have faithfully supported this ministry and our growth. We have seen God do miracles these last years, and often those miracles came through the generous donations of our friends. Thank you.

May God add His blessings and favor to all of the above who love and support me, my staff and the ministry of Teen Challenge.

Contents

Introduction

Looking back over the challenges in my life, I have noticed that the more impossible an undertaking looked, the greater I could witness the handiwork of God. When I was asked to serve as executive director of Teen Challenge of Florida, I experienced a ministry in severe crisis. Problems existed in every area of the organization and hope for solving these problems and making the necessary changes seemed slim. However, accepting the challenge, through faith and hard work, my staff and I have watched the ministry grow from thirty-six male and female students living in a rented, understaffed facility to twenty centers with highly efficient staff with housing for over a thousand students.

So many times of unprecedented problems and struggles nearly destroyed my hope of building this work, but with every trial, God came through with supernatural favor that sustained us and enabled us to grow at a steady pace. One encounter that remains fresh in my remembrance was the time that I received a call from the owner of the property we were renting for our Teen Challenge men. He explained that he wanted to redevelop the rental property and we had sixty days to move out. I will never forget his words, "I'm constructing a modular home park and golf course. The bulldozers will be there in four weeks to begin knocking down trees and then demolish the buildings. You have to get out." Get out? Get out and go where? We had no place to go. I had been searching for land and a center for Teen Challenge for some time and nothing I had found was zoned right, priced right or met the needs of a residential program.

All I knew to do at that time was to pray. I asked God for a miracle, and did He ever give me one! An eagle landed on the rental property right in the middle of the acreage that was to be developed. The owner called and said, "Jerry, you have more time. We had an eagle land, and it has stopped all development at this time." The laws that protected that eagle protected Teen Challenge and halted the plans of the developer!

That eagle bought us an additional year of time. In fact, almost one year to the day, lightning struck the tree where the eagle lived and burned it to the ground. The eagle moved out and the bulldozers moved in. The following day, there were bulldozers on the property knocking down every tree standing on the five hundred acres. And then the anticipated call followed, "Jerry, you have sixty days to be out." We had realized that sooner or later, depending on the habitation patterns of our beloved bird, we would be forced out; so, my staff and I had been pursuing property since that first call. In fact, we had transferred the women's home to another rental facility, but we had not found an appropriate location for our men. We were not sure what to do or where we could send our men since many were just coming off drugs and were in no shape to be released from the program.

Our annual staff retreat was scheduled the weekend after this call. Needless to say, the entire staff was under extreme pressure, and we had no idea what any of the team would do if forced to close the home. The situation looked bleak. But in spite of the dilemma we faced, and honestly not knowing what I would say to them, I made the decision to continue the plans for the retreat.

The second morning there, I rose early to take a jog on the beach. I had almost completed my run when I felt the tears. I was at the end of my rope and I knew it. I collapsed on the sand and began to cry out in earnest as a succession of despairing questions raced through my mind. "God," I appealed, "why did you bring me down to Florida to die?" I had done all I knew how, and in anguish I shouted out to God, "Why haven't we found a home for Teen Challenge? What do you want from me? What am I to do? What am I missing? What can I do to meet this need?" I understood that if He didn't do something, we would have to close the men's home!

Then within my spirit, I heard the still small voice of God prompt me, "Read about Isaac's wells." I wanted to say, "Excuse me, God, what do Isaac's wells have to do with my problems? I don't even remember where it is in the Bible." I assume in my frantic condition, I had hoped for a more lightning bolt direction, and I wanted to question God on His responses to my pleas and doubts, but I didn't. I returned to the house, reached for my Bible, and looked up the story. And to my amazement, God's words began to click in my spirit, and the significance of Isaac's wells began to make sense. God had my attention.

Living in a land ruled by the Philistines, Isaac was repeatedly being told to move on! As soon as he dug his first well, the shepherds of *Gerar* began to quarrel with him over it. He named this well *Esek*, which means *strife* and moved on. Isaac then dug a second well; and again, those same shepherds of *Gerar* began to quarrel. This time Isaac named the second well *Sitnah*, which means *continued strife,* and he was on his way. Not giving up, Isaac dug a third well. The Bible says no one quarreled over it; so, he named it *Rehoboth*, which means *God has given us room to spread out, and we will flourish in the land.* Finally! Revelation!

Isaac's trek to locate a home for his family encountered numerous setbacks. Just as Isaac's attempt to dig and relocate at the first well fell through, the Lord reminded me that our first attempt to purchase a building had fallen through due to quarreling with the neighborhood over zoning. Our second endeavor ended in much the same way as Isaac's second well. An attempt to buy church property brought such quarreling among the church board that we "threw in the towel" and just walked away. However, Isaac's third attempt brought success, and he settled in an area promised to bring increase and provision. As with Isaac, God promised me that He had a *Rehoboth* for Teen Challenge. My heart and spirit leaped!

For the next few days, I rested on the promise that God was going to provide us with a place to spread out and one in which we would flourish. And that was enough. Within thirty days, we purchased an office complex valued at over one million dollars. The cost to us: $440,000. Within an incredibly short time, we moved into our first men's facility, a 32,000 square foot residence! That was the beginning for Teen Challenge of Florida/Georgia. Since that time, we have grown into one of the largest networks of Teen Challenge centers in the world reaching thousands of individuals seeking help with life-controlling problems.

The next few pages unfold my personal story of God's love and compassion for hurting people. Our unlimited miracles are recorded, and I share the continued favor that surrounds the growth and ministry of Teen Challenge of Florida/Georgia. God has given us room to spread out and flourish into Southern Georgia, Kansas City, Missouri, the Caribbean, and other parts of the world. He keeps blessing, and we keep receiving, and in turn, we bless those who so urgently rely on the help Teen Challenge provides.

Throughout this journey, in my longing to do the will of God and create a ministry of excellence, God has taught me valuable leadership principles. Many of these principles were learned through experience, and others by seeking the direction of those who had gone before me. I don't claim to be an expert in building an organization, but rather, during the process, God helped me develop some guidelines that fostered solid growth for our ministry. Teen Challenge continues to learn daily, constantly working to find better means in reaching the lost and helping the hurting. As you live out your God-given destiny, I pray these principles will serve as a blueprint for following His will for your life.

Principle 1:

THE LEADER MUST
HEAR FROM GOD

No strategy, no guideline, no "how-to book," no advice from the most influential CEO is as important as hearing the voice of God. If you are developing a new ministry, church or business, hearing from God and knowing that you have heard from God are essentials to employing God's will and in getting you through the "tough times."

The dream God gives you during prayer and the call that comes from God are what keep you afloat through the storms of problems that will turn up to confront you. The call of God will keep you firmly founded in the face of doubters. The call of God will keep you expectant when there is no money. Your call will keep you encouraged when the zoning board rejects you or informs you about the overwhelming impact fees owed for building your new facility. And your call of God will keep you positive when some environmentalist proposes a block to your project in order to save some near-extinct bug, frog or cricket.

Your call will keep you when the church support can't be found. Your call is foremost and at times is your only surety; before launching out into some endeavor, be certain that He is indeed the one who has called you. You want to know that it is God who has given you the dream. Recognize that God is your source and that He is there to take you to the next level for completing the vision He has positioned for you. Investing time on your knees and on your face before God, clearly waiting for His direction, is where He will confirm the steps to attaining your dream.

Throughout my experience, God has allowed my dreams and visions to be challenged in ways that made it appear impossible to accomplish. God brings into play all types of situations to get us to trust and depend upon Him, and He often strips us of all our pride and brings us to a place where we are broken, ready to totally give up, a place where we are finally ready to completely rely on Him.

Paul Yonggi Cho said, "Never trust a man who doesn't walk with a limp." Dr. Cho's statement speaks of the brokenness we experience as we encounter life's difficult situations, but as we know, God never puts on us more than we can handle, and in the midst of all the conflict, chaos and confusions, God protects us and we survive. Our survival speaks of that quality within a person's character that is developed and polished through the pain. We learn, but we walk with a limp, a little bit wiser and a bit more dependent on God. I began to walk with a limp.

Leaders often endure difficult challenges while pursuing their dreams. Sometimes it may seem your vision or dream has died, and then, at just the right moment, God comes on the scene and brings your dream to life. This observation is no surprise to those of us who have planted a new church, started a new business, or developed a non-profit ministry. Let me share with you how God called me to the work of Teen Challenge. From this call I heard from God: somewhat reluctantly, I beckoned the call and set out to accomplish the dream God was burning within me. For the duration of this process, I knew I had to hear from Him and Him alone.

Have you ever received one of those phone calls that seemed to totally change the direction of your life? A call that challenged you with a seemingly impossible task? A call that asked you to give up everything you had worked for years to build? A call that sent you into emotional shock? A call that you deemed in the beginning couldn't possibly be God? But a call you just couldn't feel a release to bypass altogether?

While serving as pastor of a church in Conway, Arkansas, I received just such a call. And that call began a series of the most challenging yet opportune experiences of my life. From these core challenges, God proved Himself in ways I had never experienced or imagined.

My secretary buzzed me one day and said, "Pastor, you've got a call on line one. It's a Mr. Bob Manderscheid." Bob was a member of the Board of Directors of Teen Challenge Florida. I had become acquainted with him a few years earlier while serving as a youth pastor in the church he attended.

"Jerry, I'd like to ask you to consider serving in the position of executive director for Teen Challenge of Florida. I believe you're the man for the job. Every time I pray, I feel God directing me to you."

I said, "Bob, I love you, man, but I'm not even going to pray about it. I don't feel the timing is right, and I don't feel God is in this kind of a move for me. Thanks, but no thanks."

Years earlier I had worked with David Wilkerson, the founder of Teen Challenge, setting up crusades in large auditoriums, organizing outreaches in inner-city areas around the country, and teaching in his staff training school. My wife and I had also opened a home for women with addiction problems in Miami. So, I had a heart for the work of Teen Challenge, but I didn't feel the slightest interest or sensing that this position was for me.

To make a move at that time would have been very difficult, and besides, I was busy serving God and felt I was in His perfect will and I was very content serving as the pastor of the church in Arkansas. Fully committed to the church and a vision for reaching the lost in that community, my wife and I were just beginning to discern that our efforts and hard work were making a difference. The church had grown dramatically in size over the past three and a half years, and we had just completed the building of a new sanctuary and office complex. I was positive this was where God wanted my family, and probably for quite some time. The timing was not right to make any kind of move. The church had gone into debt to build, and I felt responsible to assist them in getting the debt paid.

In addition to building a new church, we also had designed and built our own new home, one intended for our specific life styles and one in which we were immeasurably enjoying. My wife, Libby, had hand selected all the wallpaper, designed the layout of each room and had her kitchen arranged and stocked just the way she wanted it. We were happy in Conway, Arkansas. We were happy in that beautiful town located at the base of the Ozark Mountains.

The families in our church were loving people who knew how to support and show appreciation to their pastor. Nearly every Sunday, my family and I would get into the car following the service to find fresh homegrown vegetables, a homemade pecan pie, or better yet, my weakness, buttermilk fudge. In fact, I made a point to never lock the doors on my car when we were at church. I never knew what gifts we might have waiting for us after a Sunday service, and I wanted to make certain they found their way to the intended receiver – me!

Why would we ever want to leave? Why would God want us to move? We were happy! We enjoyed our ministry in Conway. So I told Bob, "No! I'm not interested."

Bob kept calling! Every three or four weeks the phone would ring and I would hear, "Every time I pray, God keeps leading me back to you, Jerry."

I kept telling him, "No."

He kept calling and calling, and I kept saying, "No! No! No! Look for someone else. Please quit calling me! Bob, get the message: I'm not interested, look elsewhere."

How impossible it seemed that God would ask my family to even consider making a change with all that we had going on in our lives and ministry. I was fulfilled, working hard to build the church and following what I believed to be God's will. Our congregation was active in a statewide evangelism and new church-planting effort. The vision for the church I was pastoring was solid and there were many projects we were working on. Busy doing God's will, I felt assured I was in the right place at the right time.

For eight months in a row, Bob kept calling always sharing the same words, "Every time I pray, God leads me back to you, Jerry."

Finally, in September of 1990, he called and said, "Jerry, we are needing some help deciding exactly how to position Teen Challenge. We have to relocate the facility and need help making some decisions regarding the future of Teen Challenge. Would you and Libby come down to Winter Haven for a couple of days and help us think through some things? No commitment necessary. Just consultation work! I'll fly you down first class and take care of all your expenses while you're here."

I knew better, but a trip to Florida sounded good and I had no intention of doing anything but assisting them in a few decisions. Libby and I flew into Tampa and were driven to Winter Haven where the Teen Challenge center was located. We left the main highway to drive down Tilden Road, a bumpy two-mile stretch through orange groves that took us to the old Tilden Estate, the rental facility Teen Challenge was occupying as its center.

I'll never forget the first moments there! Both the men's and women's homes were located on the same property. The big house was in ill repair—screens rusted, paint peeling, and splotches of different colored paint splattered the brick exterior of the house. The lovely place that had once existed was now surrounded with dump-worthy junk and covered with a chalky dust and a mold that crept and climbed in every available crevice and corner. Knee high weeds grew just yards from the house and the once-upon-a-time swimming pool lay stagnant, black and dingy—a home to an amphibian assortment of turtles and frogs. The moss that hung from the massive oaks set the appropriate scene for the haunting remnants of this estate!

To the right of the big house was a worn-down modular home in need of major repair. Bob said, "Let's take a brief tour of the business office, and then we'll attend the chapel service." Unfortunately, the business office was that rundown trailer. The door leading into the office desperately needed to be replaced; it was so rotted at the bottom that if a large rat ran under it, he wouldn't have to duck his head. The door wobbled on its hinges as I opened it, and I stood in shock as I looked into the first room and saw what appeared to be an enormous oil spill. In the middle of the living area, a big glob of fresh oil was entangled and absorbed within the fibers of the gold shag carpet. Apparently someone had attempted to change the oil in his motorcycle or lawn mower without concern for mess or cleanup. Not one window in this trailer would close all the way and the bathroom toilets were out of order. The office furniture was old and worn out. And from the business end, the entire computer system for the office consisted of one 10-megabyte hard drive and one 20-megabyte hard drive. All their records were stored on these two computers. I found it impossible to believe this was the extent of their office equipment. The floor of the trailer was soft in some places; and if you stepped in the right spot, I was sure you could fall through. The smell of mildew pervaded the place and the scattered remains of dead bugs added a creepy movie touch. And that was the office complex for the executive director and administrator.

Upon completing the tour of the administration trailer, we were asked to join the students in the women's home where a room had been designated for use as a chapel. The Teen Challenge choir was set to sing for us, and a couple of students were asked to give their testimonies. I sat in a chair that was falling apart. Dried foam bulged from the ripped vinyl and the seat felt that at any moment it might give way under my weight. Of course, most all of the other seats were in similar condition.

Looking around the room, I noticed several windows were broken out, the walls needed paint and the floor needed waxed. I remember asking myself, "Why don't they fix these things? Why doesn't somebody do something about this mess?" The ceiling sagged as thick mold oozed out of its hairline cracks, the result of a leak that had not been attended. I feared it would cave-in at any moment.

In spite of the rundown environment, the sweet presence of the chapel made me forget the insufferable surroundings. I watched a group of students make their way to the front of the place of worship and begin singing. The lively, heart-felt songs permeated the entire room. Looking at each of them, I saw a glow, a sense of happiness. Change had taken place in their lives. They had met Jesus. Their faces beamed with a joy and hope that emanated their new-found freedom in Christ. They were not distracted by their surroundings as I had been.

One of the young women looked familiar, I knew her but I couldn't recall her name or even where it was that I had made her acquaintance. While searching my memory for her name, and continuing to listen, I began to sense the touch of God. His warmth came over me. My eyes welled with tears as I sat and listened. Two or three students shared moving testimonies on how drugs had wrecked their lives and how the power and love of Christ had set them free. The students sang another song, and the girl I had recognized stepped to the front and began to share her story. She explained, "I'm Megan. I'm 16 years old, and I've been in Teen Challenge for eight months."

Megan began to share how she had been physically and sexually violated. She told how her father had always lived a crazy life, abusing alcohol and drugs and that she had turned to drugs and alcohol herself to cover the pain of her early years. Tears ran down her face as she looked at me and said, "But now that I'm at Teen Challenge, Jesus has set me free." Then it came to me. Megan had lived in an apartment just a few doors down from us when we were youth pastors in Ft Myers, Florida. In fact, she had served as our baby sitter a couple of times. When the singing was over, Libby and I made our way to her and embraced her and encouraged her to stay true to her commitment to the Lord. Today, Megan is happily married and has children of her own. She calls from time to time, most often recommending some young girl she hopes to get into our program.

A tour of the women's home left me with a similar impression as that of the administrative office. I was distraught; everywhere I looked the needs were overwhelming. Bunk beds were used and falling apart and tattered mattresses were covered with faded-thin blankets and yellowed quilts and the only other furniture were a few broken-down chests for storing clothes. Personal belongings lay piled in corners and the comforts of home were not present. The ladies' bathrooms were clammy and smelled of mildew and none of the residential quarter was air-conditioned, which left all the rooms stale and muggy.

My compassion reached out for the women and I tried to encourage as many of the students as I could during the tour. Yet, I felt a bit guilty knowing I was leaving to return to a cozy home, while they would continue to live under the severe nauseating surroundings.

After leaving the chapel, we walked up the long, dusty road back to the men's home to tour that facility and meet several of the men's home staff. They were showing signs of burnout, pain, disillusionment, but, most of all, fear. I was guided through the men's dorm and the staff rooms only to witness much of the same conditions as I had found in the women's dorms. The beat-up furniture and old Lazy Boy chairs in every room were all broken-down and soiled. The reoccurring question kept surfacing in my mind, "Why do they keep this place so crowded, run-down and messy?" Again the thought hit me, "Somebody ought to do something about this mess."

During the tour I met many committed staff members who had served faithfully in these tough circumstances, the most memorable being the intake coordinator, a former Elvis impersonator. I remember so vividly walking into his office, sitting down on his broken-down couch, and my posterior hitting the floor. My knees were up under my chin, and I was looking up at this big husky fellow who was the spitting image of Elvis. I couldn't help but think, "He's alive. Elvis is alive. I found him hiding in the orange groves in Florida. He's had a bad LSD trip and doesn't know who he is."

This fellow had quite the assortment of religious paraphernalia all over his desk. Bumper stickers covered the front and items such as a Plexiglas ark of the covenant he had gotten from Jimmy Swaggart adorned the top. He said to me as I chatted with him, "When I leave Teen Challenge, I'm leaving in a body bag." I thought about that for a moment and decided I didn't want to mess with Elvis. Later, I found out that he had come to Teen Challenge with a .357 pistol with intentions of killing anyone he could and then killing himself. He had given up on life and had no desire to live. Instead, he ended up giving his life to Christ, completing the Teen Challenge program, and had worked his way up to being a staff member. God's grace had gotten him through his past.

Another interesting staff member I met that day was very excited about showing me his chickens; the only unusual thing about this situation was that he raised them in the back of his station wagon. That's right—you read it correctly—he raised chickens in his car. Straw, water, and chicken manure were added accessories to his vehicle. However, he was sincere in his work, had a devout love for the students and took great care of his chickens!

Can you picture how these circumstances affected me? The entire ministry, its buildings, its staff, and its problems were overwhelming. I couldn't imagine how any one ministry could have so many different areas needing attention, and I couldn't imagine dealing with all those needs. In order to help you appreciate the challenge at that time, a few of the issues plaguing the ministry are listed below:

Previous leaders had compromised their morals
Staff members were burnt out and hurting
Staff had not been paid for months
Most of the staff had no formal training
Questions surrounded some of the current staff
Office equipment was outdated and inefficient
Buildings were dilapidated and in ruin
Students were challenged with mental problems
Vehicles were broken down
Tons of furniture needed replaced
No solid fundraisers were in position
No goals or visions were articulated
The Board of Directors consisted of only two members
Public image of the ministry was shattered

To top it all off, the owner of the property had given Teen Challenge a notice that soon they would need to move out of these leased facilities! As I mentioned in the Introduction, the property was going to be developed into a golf course and modular home project. What an impossible situation! As I walked the grounds, just remembering what I was experiencing, made me shudder, and I kept trying to remind myself that they had asked me to come only as a consultant.

That evening, Bob asked us to dinner to discuss the ministry and its needs. The meal was wonderful and the fellowship was great, but I was careful not to lead him to believe that I was remotely interested in being a part of the solution for Teen Challenge. He asked us to please prayerfully consider the position and reminded me again that God had told him that I was the one for the position. Assuring Bob that we would pray, Libby and I went back to the hotel. It was obvious to both of us that something needed to be done. Teen Challenge needed a leader. We felt true compassion for the situation but were convinced that we were not the ones they were looking for. God was using us in Conway and we were happy. Surely God must have someone else in mind, so I went to bed convinced that I would not be open to the executive director position.

At 5:00 a.m. the next morning I awoke to a familiar voice. God was speaking to me. I rolled over in bed and pushed a pillow over my head, hoping that would quiet the voices in my head. But, I kept picturing the faces of the students singing and sharing testimonies. I fought to go back to sleep, but kept tossing and turning as His Spirit continued to speak to me. Then, I knew I had to answer the urge I sensed in my heart.

Slipping into the bathroom so I wouldn't awaken my wife, I sat down on the floor between the toilet and the bathtub. How strange it is that we come face to face with God in some of the most unusual places. The floor was cool and hard, but it was private and the place where God wanted me for the moment. I began to wait on the Lord in quiet worship and I whispered praises, remaining sensitive to His voice. I kept thinking of Megan and prayed for her and the other students. I finally conceded, "God, I know You're here. I know You're wanting to speak to me. I'm listening."

In my heart I was hoping He was not going to ask me to take the job with Teen Challenge. Prayerfully and respectfully I said, "If You're wanting me to come to Florida Teen Challenge, You are going to have to give me clear direction in Your Word. I am not going to let my emotions lead me. Lord, where do You want me to read? What are you saying, God?"

In just a matter of moments, the voice in my spirit instructed, "Read the book of Nehemiah." The message was so loud and clear it might as well have been audible. On hearing this I thought, "Oh, no!" I know what Nehemiah says and I wasn't sure I wanted to read Nehemiah, but nonetheless, the voice in my spirit was distinctly clear, "Read Nehemiah." I knew I had to be faithful, so I began reading.

> *Hanani, one of my brothers, came from Judah with some other men, and I questioned them about the remnant that survived the exile, and also about Jerusalem. They said to me, "Those who survived the exile*

and are back in the province are in great
trouble and disgrace. The wall of Jerusalem
is broken down, and its gates have been
burned with fire. (Nehemiah 1:2-3, NIV)

The situation taking place in the first few chapters of
Nehemiah goes something like this: the enemy was coming and going as they pleased and taking what they wanted from God's people. God sent a few friends to Nehemiah to tell him about the condition of the people of Israel
and He spoke to him through the words of these men. The
wall of Jerusalem was in shambles and God told Nehemiah to go and rebuild the wall. Notice in the first four chapters, there was no audible voice, no angel appearing, no
burning bush, no cloud to follow—all Nehemiah heard
was the message that his people were in trouble. They were
in need, and God used their need to challenge Nehemiah to
take action. In essence, the need was the call.

When Sanballat heard that we were rebuild-
ing the wall, he became angry and was
greatly incensed. He ridiculed the Jews, and
in the presence of his associates and the
army of Samaria, he said, "What are those
feeble Jews doing? Will they restore their
wall? Will they offer sacrifices? Will they fin-
ish in a day? Can they bring the stones back
to life from those heaps of rubble—burned as
they are?" (Nehemiah 4:1-2, NIV).

Sanballat and Tobiah were mocking Nehemiah and
God's people. What arrogance! What a proud statement!

How could these guys mock God's people by questioning His power? My eyes began to fill with tears as I began to sense God speaking to me. Faith spoke up, "Yes, they *can*. They *can* be restored! Those burned-over stones in God's hands can be used to rebuild the wall. The burned-over rubble is usable in God's hands. Yes, God can do it!"

Then the Lord began to open my eyes and show me what He wanted me to see from this story. The Lord told me the broken-down walls reflected the state of the Teen Challenge ministry in Florida—broken down, the enemy coming and going as he pleased, causing overwhelming grief and financial problems. The enemy was mocking Teen Challenge. The staff members, similar to the people of Israel, were beaten down and broken spirited—with no hope, no sense of direction; they lived in fear and lament. God told me the burned-over stones were representative of the broken lives—burned out, burned over, with very little apparent worth. But God shared that He could change them, that He could and can restore those stones to life. Drug addicts can be set free!

I heard His spirit well up in me, "I want you to help rebuild the walls of this ministry." God spoke to me to move to Florida. I prayed. I read. I prayed again. Then I reread the first five chapters of Nehemiah, hoping I could convince myself that I was not hearing God correctly. I finally left the bathroom and crawled back into bed. Libby asked, "Are you okay?"

Uncertain if I were okay, I answered with all the enthusiasm I could muster, "Sure, dear!" We relaxed a while longer and then rose for the day.

When I got up, I began thinking of all that we had in Arkansas, all we would have to give up, all the friends we'd have to bid goodbye, and I certainly didn't want to make a hasty decision. Was I willing to commit to do what I knew the Lord was asking of me? I had no answer, and at that time, I decided not to say anything to Libby. I didn't have to.

Knowing that I was experiencing the aftermath of shock at what we had witnessed at the center and discerning the burden in my heart, Libby asked, "What are you feeling, Jerry?"

I actually did not know. My heart was hurting; my mind was swirling and my spirit was preparing me. "I don't know," I responded. "I need to spend some time in prayer."

At our visit, Libby did not feel that the Lord was directing her to become involved. Her loyalty and concern was for our church and congregation in Conway and before she even would think about Teen Challenge, she wanted the assurance from God that He had a plan for the church, which would not rely on our involvement. And although Libby, as I, had been greatly moved by what we had seen and was burdened to pray for Teen Challenge, she didn't think we were the ones to lead the ministry.

That morning Bob took us to breakfast and showed us around the grounds and area some more. He asked us over and over again what we were feeling. We both assured him we would pray about the situation and let him know within one month.

We headed back home. Feeling guilty for even considering leaving our church, I kept telling myself to remember that we had just built the new building and office complex. Surely that wasn't God speaking; it must have been my emotional concern for the staff and students in Teen Challenge, but nothing more. We were enjoying our home that we had built just two years earlier, the kids were in great schools, our church congregants were good people and I worked with a first-rate, highly competent deacon board. Outside the church, I had been offered several opportunities to speak in other ministries and churches and recently I had been asked to serve as the director of a special statewide church-planting project. My life was good. We had it made.... so to speak. We were happy where we were. Why would we move?

Upon returning, I went right back to work in the church like everything was business as usual. But soon, a real problem developed. Every time I knelt to pray, the Lord would remind me that He was calling me to Florida. In fact, God clearly spoke to me to move to Orlando and relocate the Teen Challenge ministry to that area. I would answer, "Okay," in my prayer time and then I would get up, look around and say, "No way, Lord. We're happy here. My kids are settled in school; the church is growing. Surely, You can use someone else. Please, Lord, send someone else. I know You can't be finished with me here."

But each time I prayed, He'd say "go" and I'd say "yes." Then I'd get up, think about my current life and doubt God's will. I came to the point where I just wouldn't pray. I didn't want to hear God's direction. Imagine that! A pastor preaching, teaching classes and counseling, but without prayer! I was miserable and so were the folks seeking counsel and ministry from me.

One month went by, then two, and I wouldn't make the commitment. Finally, the burden to be in God's will was so great, and I was so unhappy that I said, "Yes." But my dear wife Libby had not gotten that release! She knew I had heard the call, and she knew God was talking to her; but she was struggling with leaving the security of our home and church, and she didn't want to hurt our congregation or our dear friends in any way. In the past, we'd always practiced praying through until we knew without a doubt what to do. We had never been afraid of doing God's will, whatever it might be. We had always followed Him, but this time it was much more difficult—the church, the people, the house, the schools, and the security – a life we cherished and loved.

One day Libby was busy at work in her kitchen when the Lord showed up. God began to confirm that He was calling us to Florida, assuring her He was in control. He told her, "It won't be easy, but it will be worth it." Libby began to glance around her kitchen—the wallpaper that she had chosen, the matching curtains, the cabinets she had selected personally, but God softly told her to let it go. She came to my office where I was studying. With tears in her eyes she said, "I'm ready to go now. I know we must go!" She mentioned that the Lord had said the move would be hard, but would be worth it. How blessed I am to have a wonderful wife who knows when God has spoken and is willing to let go and do His will. We hugged and cried together.

Those days were difficult, looking at our friends and church members and knowing we were about to leave them weighed on us heavily. The special folk at Conway loved us; they loved our children; they invited us to their homes for meals and times of fellowship. How could we hurt them? How could we leave them when we had worked so hard together to build the new sanctuary? They had followed the vision God had given us for the church and had been wonderful servants. But that part of my life was over; God was birthing in me a new vision, and I could no longer resist God's will for my life.

Telling my friends that God was calling me to Orlando was one of the most difficult tasks I've ever had to carry out. It's so difficult for church boards and church family to agree with you or God when you tell them He has spoken to you to leave them. Their feelings of love for you always seem to get in the way of being able to believe it was really God.

Christmas time had always been special in Conway. Each year, we invited the Board and their families to our home and bought gifts to express our appreciation for their support and ministry in the church. They, too, always brought us special gifts for our home and blessed us, but this time it was different. The Christmas gifts became parting gifts; we were saying our goodbyes. And because we loved them so much, it was especially uncomfortable.

The next few weeks were filled with salty tears, warm words, and farewells. The Conway closure wasn't easy and thoughts often interrupted my vision with, "You're crazy, you're an idiot, what are you doing? You are making the biggest mistake of your life."

My mom, who lives in Arkansas, said, "I guess in our lifetime, we'll never see you live close to us again." She didn't mean to add pressure on us, but I couldn't help but feel guilty for leaving them as well. We packed the house, the movers loaded us up, and we were on our way.

There is a price to pay to be a leader and to do God's will. And sometimes that price seems higher than we think it will be. John Maxwell said, "To get up you must first give up." Then he said, "To stay up you must give up more." Are you willing to step up to the next level? Are you willing to pay the price? To complete the dream God has given you will require that you die to yourself. Your wife, husband or family may not understand, but you must take the lead, pray for your family's support and press on until your dream becomes real. You must see it; you must believe it, and you must work as though its manifestation is just around the corner. Many have quit just before their dream actualizes and they claim, "I can't take any more; it shouldn't be so hard; God is not with me," and they give up. Don't give up, and don't let your current situation dictate your future.

During the next few chapters, I will reveal some of the most challenging events of my life and disclose how God led me through each and every one of them. I'm thankful God gave us the grace to persist and pursue and see His dream become a certainty in our lives. Listen for God's voice. Hear from God. Be willing to accept the call and God will do the rest.

Principle 2:

PRAY HARD, WORK HARD
THEN PRAY GOD
BLESSES YOUR WORK

The starting point of any ministry or business is prayer. Prayer is where you get the necessary guidance for every day direction. E.M Bounds said, *"Prayer is power; more prayer means more power."*

Prayer opens you to God's influence and gives you divine guidance as to how He wants you to fulfill the dream He has placed inside you. God rarely allows us to see very far down the road of our future walk. He tends to give us only the enlightenment needed to take one step at a time, do one task at a time, one year at a time. Yet prayer is where you get the confirmation and inspiration, by His Spirit, to walk on or to take the next step.

Pray hard! A leader's prayer life is key to successfully completing his God-given destiny. You must, without exception, maintain an active prayer life, as your prayer life is the measure of your dependence on Him. Many leaders speak of getting up early in the morning to pray before their day begins, and others say they spend their time with God late into the evenings. It's not about when you take the time to be with God, but it is a matter of *do you take time with God?*

I find that I need to spend time in prayer in the mornings before the day gets too hectic and the demands of others distract me from my devotions. But when there are key decisions or issues to deal with, I take time to pray throughout the entire day. For instance, I may have my secretary hold calls for an hour or two, or I may take the afternoon off to go to a secret place to pray. Actually, you can talk to God anywhere. I have had great conversations with Him while driving my car, riding in an elevator, or even sitting in a courtroom waiting to be called for testimony in some case for which I am involved. The key is that you make prayer a priority in developing your vision. Hear from God, keep your prayer life current, and then go to work. God has always used people to fulfill His will. He will do His part; He just wants you to do yours. And your part begins with prayer.

Work Hard! I can't tell you how many times I've heard sincere people say that they are waiting on God to tell them what to do next, when in fact, they are doing nothing. Many have received extensive educations, talked about what they felt God might want them to do, but then they do nothing. They are not assisting with any ministry, not working in the field of expertise in which they are trained and they seem to think that their harvest will be lain at their feet or fall into place without any effort on their part.

Waiting lazily on God is not the way to reach your goals! God always qualifies those He calls; but then God expects them to apply themselves and get busy serving, or God's obligation ceases. Whether you are called by God to work in a non-profit ministry, or workplace ministry, the road to success and promotion is sustaining the heart of a servant. I have always believed that a person should just get busy serving in any place they are needed. Many times the *need* is the call. If your church or any non-profit organization needs help, volunteer. Try asking your pastor or a community leader in what ways you can help. Regardless of the work, regardless of the need, say *yes*. Tell him, *"I will do it."* Serve, serve, serve, and your gifts will always make a place for you. Serving will allow your leadership skills to increase, and God will make His will much easier to understand.

Work Smart! God wants you to be diligent in your work habits, but I also want to remind you to work smart. Digging a ditch is hard work, but if you dig the ditch in the wrong place, then your work has been done in vain. Work smart. If you have a plan where the ditch is needed and follow the plan, then the ditch will be in the right place with the least amount of effort. If you are going to sweat, rub blisters, and exert valuable time getting them, you might as well accomplish the intended task. If you dig the ditch in the right place the first time, you only have to dig it once. Smart? Common sense? Sometimes in our world, *common sense is not so common.* Time is too valuable to waste it, so picture yourself working smart by investing time in thought before taking action.

Often people set goals, and then daily challenges occupy so much of their time, they lose their sense of direction. The urgent steals the time they should have invested in bringing their plans to completion. They wake up one day and ask, "Where did all the time go?" And they settle for average. Rather than breaking the bad habit of allowing distractions to dominate and sidetrack them, they leave their dream behind in the ashes of a busy life. Busy is not always best, especially if you are not staying true to your life goals.

The greatest thief of time is people. They don't mean to distract you from your work, but they do. Set goals for the day and stay focused. Schedule time to see people but limit the time, and be prepared to say to an uninvited guest, "I have five minutes, but if that isn't enough time, we can get together another day."

Working hard reveals character. Whether you are working in a workplace or non-profit organization, whether employer or employee, those around you are watching. How many hours you work, how hard you work, and how focused you are, speak volumes to your followers. You can't build a ministry or a business sitting around an office expecting others to come to you. You can't raise funds for your operations, or capital for projects, sitting around. Be a leader in your work ethic. Set the pace, and others will follow. I encourage my staff to set the standard for those working with them and for them. When one of them takes the students in our program out for a work project, I expect the staff member to set the pace and be the example. Be a leader. Don't just boss everyone around and stand in the shade sipping lemonade; pick up a shovel and get that ditch dug. No one is more highly respected than the leader who works alongside those he leads.

Ask God to bless your work! Pray hard, work hard, work smart, and finally, ask God to bless your work. Your goal should begin with prayer and end with prayer. Your plans and hard work should be sandwiched between prayer, therefore increasing your chances of success. I am convinced that we have unlimited ideas that have not been bathed in prayer, and as a result, they don't produce the outcomes we hope for. I challenge you to pray, and then follow your vision. See God's faithfulness in converting your dreams to reality.

After we heard from God and prayed through to find His perfect will, my wife and I went to work. We resigned the church pastorate and put our house up for sale. On January 15, 1991, my family set out on the journey to Orlando. We made it as far as Pensacola, Florida, the first day. The next day we were off to Orlando, following God's will for our family. We pulled up to our rented house in Orlando the next evening, tired, but relieved to be home. Unfortunately, our furniture was a couple of days behind us. Our kids thought that was great, "Let's just camp out here, Dad." So we got out our sleeping bags and did just that. What a terrific evening and a positive experience for our kids their first night in Orlando! Even our neighbor's kids came over and stayed one night while we waited for our furniture to arrive. They gave the kids a complete rundown on how to have fun in their new neighborhood. We had prayed that God would give them new friends, and He met that need the first day we arrived.

The furniture came, we unpacked, and I began the task of rebuilding the walls of the Teen Challenge ministry. Even though I wasn't sure where to begin, I did know one thing; I was in God's will and I could pray again and not feel guilty!

The center was located in Winter Haven, a one-hour-and-fifteen-minute drive - *if* the traffic didn't get backed up. This travel time became precious to me; I talked to God, enjoyed inspired ministry via cassette tape, and most importantly, listened to God as He prepared me for the days and months ahead. In the natural, everything was in such a mess that it was hard to know where to begin, so I had to lean heavily on God for direction.

Teen Challenge had no plan, no strategy, and no goals. The staff had no heart to even continue. They had just given up. They didn't trust me, and to them, I was just another leader talking big dreams that seemed impossible to fulfill. It was time to go to work. Lots of prayer, long hours of hard work and more prayer is where I began.

Although I am painting a bleak picture, the facts were the facts. Every team member had lost hope. For months I sensed they were afraid of me but could not pinpoint the reason behind the fear. Then one day while I was meeting with one of the maintenance staff, he looked at me and asked, "Are you planning to fire us all?" Now, I had discovered the reason behind the fear! One of the departing leaders had been circulating rumors that I was going to fire the entire staff and that they should be looking for other jobs. No wonder they were all afraid of me. That day, team building made a small step in the right direction with my assurance that we were all in this "thing" together!

The lease on the Teen Challenge facility in Winter Haven was up, and we had no place to relocate. I had no idea what to do but pray, work hard and trust God to handle all the details. The Board told me to not worry about locating a building because they had someone working on it and was sure he would find what we needed. They told me, "You just worry about the program and fundraising." The Board had worked to keep the center debt free and had some savings in place to assist with the cost of operations. But those funds would only last a couple of more months, and fundraising was critical to the success of the program.

As I delved deeper into the daily operations of Teen

Challenge, I realized that not one area of the ministry had any momentum; the *"big mo"* John Maxwell talks about had long ago dried up or flown away. Getting the ministry moving in the right direction was going to take a miracle. Everything was in a mess, and it felt like all I was doing was putting out fires. Overwhelmed with frustration, I had to constantly remind myself of God's call and God's purpose.

The person the Board had assigned to look for property for us couldn't find anything that would fit into our price range and our unique zoning requirements. Becoming discouraged, he gave up and resigned his task. So, I began looking for a building to house the twenty men, twenty ladies, our staff and offices. After hundreds of hours looking at building after building—hospitals, convalescent homes, houses, churches, restaurants—we found nothing. Every facility that would meet our needs cost a million dollars plus, and all we found that we could afford were dilapidated buildings located in the wrong zoning. Tremendous pressure began to mount to find a home for Teen Challenge. My team and I were praying and believing for a property that would open soon and one that would meet our every need. The problem was, that as the saying goes, we needed it yesterday! The landlord had given us notice to relocate, and we were living on borrowed time. We had no place to go. Where would we place all these students who desperately relied on Teen Challenge? And how were we going to take care of those we presently had in our program?

When you begin the undertaking of a new ministry or rebuilding one, you will face obstacles you never dreamed existed. When this happens, keep your dreams alive by solidifying the vision in your heart and staying single minded on the desired end result. Prayer and work—hard work—is the starting point. Then you will need to address and evaluate each area of challenge. Identify the key divisions that you must tackle first and often times that pressing challenge is the need for income. You must have money to operate, and the means through which you receive money must be in place and working well before you can grow and move on to other projects.

Fundraising takes time. Fundraising is about relationships. I'm convinced there is no lack of money in God's economy; there is just a lack of relationships. Fundraising is work - *hard* work. Whether business for profit, or nonprofit ministry, many find fundraising to be the most demanding element of their job. Raising funds will test your fortitude and determination, but the rewards can be phenomenal if you work hard, work smart, and keep a good attitude. And that is where I began—praying hard, working hard, and then praying God would bless my work.

Principle 3:

CHERISH AND CELEBRATE
VICTORIES ALONG THE WAY

When you begin the work of your dream, God will reveal glimpses of what He wants to do through you. The dream may take time, but along the way God will reward your efforts with an occasional victory. Some victories are small, and some are large. Cherish them, celebrate them, remember them, and use them to remind yourself that you are on the right track. Always remember that the people you work with, the people you serve and the people who support you are the reason you are where you are. Celebrate them. Celebrate with them and share the victories along the way with them. Often, we overlook small victories and in doing so miss an opportunity to be encouraged in the Lord and to encourage others.

Your beginning days are the most difficult, but they are the days where your character is being built and some of your lifetime friendships are being formed. This is the time to look for small miracles and signs that God is indeed moving you toward the vision He has placed in your heart. During those early years when there were days I felt the vision God had given me was unattainable, wonderful victories were being played out right in front of my eyes. Let me share the testimonies of some of the lives that were changed at Teen Challenge during those initial days.

A young lady named Maurice came into the program during those challenging days of rebuilding Teen Challenge. Let me tell you that God works even in times of chaos. Maurice came to Teen Challenge at a desperate time in her life. Crack cocaine had stripped her of everything but her breath. She was skin and bones. Maurice had no idea of the internal bedlam happening at Teen Challenge. All she wanted was help with her addiction. Maurice's life started out fine; she was an honor student in high school and was even the homecoming queen. Though she was popular, making good grades and winning awards, Maurice had a dark side. At the age of fourteen, she began experimenting with marijuana and alcohol, and by the age of twenty, she had escalated to powder cocaine. Not many years later, crack cocaine became the drug that controlled her every move.

Her addiction eventually put her on the streets, homeless and hopelessly addicted. Maurice remembers telling God, "If you will give me a baby, I will stop smoking crack." After years of addiction, at the age of thirty-two, she became pregnant with Jameira. Maurice forgot her promise to God and while carrying her child, she was so bound by her addiction that she continued to smoke crack. In fact, her need for the drug kept her from getting to the hospital; her daughter was born in a 1990 Grand Am. When she did enter the emergency unit, the attendants rushed out, cut the umbilical cord, and took the baby into the hospital.

The next day social workers came into her room and told Maurice that her baby was cocaine positive and that she could not take her home. She was told one of her family members would have to be responsible for her. She asked her mother, and then her aunt, to take the baby. They refused. Human Resource Services (HRS) became involved at this point, and said the baby would have to go into foster care while Maurice entered a treatment center. Fortunately, she found a place in Jacksonville that would allow mothers to bring their children while going through treatment. In this way, Maurice was able to keep Jameira with her.

Maurice completed the program and moved to Ft. Meade, believing a new location might make a difference in her lifestyle. But, it was just a matter of time before she began smoking crack again. When forced by her case-worker to take a drug test, she failed. She was told that she needed long-term treatment, and if she did not get it, she would lose her parental rights.

Following a friend's advice, Maurice applied to Teen Challenge. She had little hope in any program changing her, but was desperate enough to try. As usual, she did everything she could think of to back out of joining the program, but her friend was at her door early the next morning, insisting she come.

Maurice was an angry, bitter woman when she arrived at the doorstep of Teen Challenge. In truth, she was mostly mad at herself for agreeing to come; she had convinced herself that she did not need long-term care. Then a staff member made a statement that was the beginning of healing and health to Maurice, "Don't just go through the program," she told her, "but try letting the program go through you." At first she didn't understand the power in that statement, or what could happen to someone who would allow the program to saturate her life, but slowly she began to yield her will. In a matter of days, Maurice committed her life to Christ.

Maurice began to memorize scripture and prepare for tests, which allowed the Word of God to become real to her. She became a role model for other students, and her leadership abilities blossomed. Other ladies in the program began coming to her for advice, and she was able to share with them how Christ had changed her life. Maurice was doing so well in the program that she was promoted to an intern. During her time at Teen Challenge, God gave Maurice a vision to open a woman's facility of her own that she was to call, "House of Israel." A short time later, she graduated and moved to Ft. Meade, Florida, and developed the House of Israel Ministry for women. I am proud of Maurice. She has her children back, is working hard, living right before the Lord, and assisting others who have life-controlling problems.

Then there's Charlotte. Charlotte is another Teen Challenge success story. Not long after I became Director of Teen Challenge, Charlotte entered the women's home. She was in horrible shape the day she came into the program. Addicted to over-the-counter drugs, Charlotte was taking up to one hundred or more Xanax tablets a day. That quantity of drugs would have killed the average person, but Charlotte had built such immunity to them that she needed that many just to sustain the high she needed to cope with life. Five different doctors in the Orlando area were prescribing these drugs to her and almost every dime she and her husband earned was being spent on drugs.

Charlotte's story is as sad as any I have ever heard. She was four when her mother left her and her two brothers at a park bench and drove away. Charlotte told us, "I remember waiting while my brothers kept assuring me that mom would be back. We played around the bus stop all day, but she never returned. Later in the evening, a police officer picked us up and took us to children and family services." She was separated from her brothers and placed in foster care.

Charlotte said, "I was in twelve different foster homes in eight years, and was sexually abused in every one of them. I didn't understand why! I didn't understand what was causing this to happen! What was I doing wrong? Why was I treated this way? When I was twelve, my mother and her new husband came to get my two brothers and me. I remember being so happy, seeing my brothers again and being with my mom. My step-dad treated us fine for about a year, and then, he started sexually abusing me. I just gave up. I started drinking and using drugs at twelve which led me to heroin addiction."

A desperate young lady, Charlotte was "looking for love in all the wrong places." At the age of thirteen, she married a fourteen-year-old heroin addict; at fifteen, she became a mother. The arrival of her son put a desire for change in Charlotte's heart; she wanted a better life for her little boy, but she just didn't know how to begin; she obviously had never had a role model or a parent who cared.

One evening, she and her husband were in a drug house that was raided by the police. Charlotte said, "I was arrested for having marijuana seeds in my possession." Because of prior trouble due to drug possession, prostitution, and other violations, this arrest would be more costly to Charlotte than she would ever have imagined. She was stunned when the judge announced her sentence, "Two years." She had been sure she would just be given another warning.

Tears ran down Charlotte's cheeks as she described her life in prison. "The first night I was sitting in my cell and four girls came to the door. They began to say things that scared me to death. I couldn't believe what was happening to me. They began to hit me and tear at my clothes. I fought back but couldn't stop them; they knocked me unconscious and raped me." Charlotte went on to say that these women abused her over and over during the next two years. Sadly, she reflected, "The only way I could deal with this mistreatment was by mentally leaving my body. I wouldn't resist, I just went on a mental trip. By the time I was released from prison, I didn't know who I was or whether I was straight or lesbian."

Charlotte's first husband divorced her while she was in prison and disappeared with their son. She spent three years and thousands of dollars looking for them, but has never seen them again. She remarried, this time to a sailor who was also a drug abuser. She gave birth to a second child, but neither the baby nor parenting responsibilities stopped her from continuing to use drugs and live an out-of-control lifestyle. Charlotte was an unfit mother, her marriage was breaking up, and she continued to have trouble with the law. Her addictive choices escalated to a new height.

Thinking if she moved that life might get better, Charlotte headed to California. She left her husband and child to chase after her addiction. Just as her first husband had done, her second divorced her and disappeared with the child. Her life was spiraling out of control. She danced in nude bars, continued to use drugs, and finally, ended up homeless, living in the streets, sleeping in cardboard boxes.

After enduring devastating conditions, Charlotte finally pulled herself out of this pit. She married the third time, trained to become a hairdresser and moved back to Orlando. During this transition, Charlotte's husband made a decision for Christ and began attending church. Wanting and trying to change, she began attending with him, but before long, her drug troubles caught up with her again, this time in the form of the prescription drug Xanax. Charlotte hid the drugs throughout their house and quickly built up tolerances, which required her to take more and more for the buzz she desired. Because of his love for Charlotte and the child born to them, her husband wanted her to get help. He knew that Charlotte's addiction was going to destroy them. Running up credit cards with one charge after another, borrowing from friends and spending every penny she could get on Xanax, Charlotte soon had her family facing financial difficulty and had herself in an unmanageable existence. Charlotte went to her church for help, and they referred her to Teen Challenge. She came just as she was, addicted, hopeless, and with a lifetime of painful memories.

I came out of my office the day Anoosh, our women's home director, was showing Charlotte around the facility. She was standing there looking worn out, tired, helpless and so very afraid. You see, she knew the pain of the detoxification process and feared she would die coming off the drugs. She worried about the unbearable cramps, the spasmodic convulsions and the severe pain associated with kicking Xanax.

But something happened. Later that day, Charlotte came into the chapel wanting help, and help she found! She met Jesus, who not only saved her, but also healed her from all the symptoms of Xanax detoxification. Because of God's grace and mercy, she had no severe withdrawal pains. God touched her, and she knew it. Praise God! What a miracle!

Charlotte worked through her numerous issues and learned a whole new way of doing life. In our one-year program, she became excited about the things God was teaching her. In addition to her healing, she served as an encouragement to the new girls who came into the program. Her story helped them realize that they hadn't had it so bad. What a joy it was to witness God heal Charlotte through the Teen Challenge Program.

Karen is another miracle that came along during the challenging times. She was forty-five when she sought the help of Teen Challenge. Now, you may be wondering why we call our program Teen Challenge when we work with both teens and adults. The answer is that as we grew, more and more drug and alcohol abusers of all ages came to us for help. Individual states began to require that you separate children under the age of eighteen from those who were eighteen or older. We were working with so many who were over the age of eighteen that we felt the need to provide programs for them as well as for the youth. So, we developed programs for boys and girls as well as programs for adult men and women.

How exciting it was to see changed lives in the middle of the craziness that was happening at Teen Challenge. Daily, we were confronted with adversity, yet we saw miracle upon miracle happen in the lives of the men and women entering the program. The victories within these individuals made our efforts worthwhile. We had much work to do with many areas of need, and many problems, yet God was helping people in spite of our struggles, in spite of the underdeveloped program and our dysfunctional staff. So, we celebrated the victories and rejoiced with those who were seeing God restore their lives and families, and we planned for the future work at Teen Challenge.

So, whether in non-profit, or workplace ministry, remember to celebrate both the small and the triumphant victories along the way. Pay attention to those who are blessed by your efforts, and use those moments as fuel for energy to continue along the path God has mapped out for you. Give praise to the staff and interns who are helping these ladies. Reflect praise to the team of workers that are making the results possible. We at Teen Challenge knew there were other men and women with similar stories to those of Maurice and Charlotte's who desperately needed Teen Challenge to stay open. They needed us to continue our efforts so they, too, could be free from substance addiction. Where were we to go? What were we to do? We didn't have a clue! But, these victories gave us the momentum to continue our journey.

Principle 4:

PRAY FOR FAVOR WITH GOD AND MAN

1991 was over! Teen Challenge of Florida had survived. But to my finite mind the challenges that loomed over the horizon were as huge as the giants Joshua and Caleb encountered when spying out Canaan. Every waking moment was taken up by one difficulty after another. Genuinely seeking God for answers, I went to the Bible where a principle began to materialize regarding God's favor.

In first Samuel 2:26 the Bible says, "Samuel grew in wisdom and stature and in favor with God and man." He not only grew in wisdom and stature as he matured, but he also grew in favor with God, and he grew in favor with man. The principle of favor became an important one in his life, as he was well received and respected as the prophet of God.

The Book of Psalms teaches us that David prayed God would give him favor with God and man. Why do you think he prayed that way? Do you think David realized the value of God's favor as well as the favor of man? Solomon identified favor with God and man being the result of love and faithfulness. And finally in Luke 2:52, we read "Jesus grew in wisdom and stature and in favor with God and man." The Bible speaks clearly on the subject of the importance of God's favor, and man's favor.

Just as the favor of the Lord was important in the lives of Biblical leaders of the past, it is just as important in the life of a leader today. In Psalm 5:12 the Bible says, "For you, oh Lord, will bless the righteous; with favor you will surround him as with a shield." Then in Psalm 30:5 it says, "His favor is for life," and in verse six, "Now in my prosperity I said, I shall never be moved." Then in verse seven, "Lord, by your favor you have made my mountain stand strong." In Proverbs 11:27 it says, "He who earnestly seeks good, finds favor."

These, and many other scriptures, show us that if we will seek God, and seek the good of others, we will find the favor of God. He desires to help each of us succeed in the dream He has given for our lives. The road may be difficult, but that is not the point. His favor is with us no matter what our circumstances may bring. He loves us and wants to fellowship with us. God's favor surrounds us and protects us like a shield. His provision is there for us, and His will is to bless us, as we are faithful to do what He has called us to do.

The second half of this principle informs us that we may also have favor with man. I had never noticed the principle in the scriptures where we could have favor with man. I saw this principle demonstrated again and again in the scriptures, and God spoke to me to begin praying for favor with both God and man, so I prayed, "Father, I want favor with You, and Father, I want favor with men."

My prayer began to develop and get more specific, "Father, give me favor with You and give me favor with men who will love Teen Challenge and give generously to help us reach our goals." Amazingly, He quickly answered that prayer.

God brought some special people into our lives who fell in love with the mission of Teen Challenge and shared their influence and affluence with us. One day a businessman walked into my office and wanted to sell me some T-shirts. God gave me favor with this man and his wife, and within a year he transferred $130,000 in stock to Teen Challenge. Praise God! Who would have thought that a T-shirt salesman would have enough money to give that kind of gift? I learned to never underestimate anyone's ability to give. God's favor and man's favor are real. This man and his wife became advisory board members and were a great blessing to us. God answered my specific prayer, and His favor made the way for man's favor.

Although obvious that God was helping us, time was running out on our lease in Winter Haven. We had no possible location to house the ministry, no place to move our students and no idea where God would take us. We needed God's favor and the favor of man desperately. Teen Challenge had to move and we needed a facility. Yes, I believed God was going to do His part, but time was running out, and I was getting a little nervous.

We had been given sixty days to relocate. A new golf course had been planned on the property we were leasing, and time was up. Then the call came. Tom Chapman, a good friend of our ministry and the owner of the property told me, "Jerry, you guys don't have to be in a rush. An eagle has landed on the property, and we can't move forward with our project until he moves."

"An eagle?" I said.

"Yes, an eagle," Tom said. "We are not able to do any construction until the eagle moves." (Federal laws prohibited any construction or development that comes within 1500 feet of the eagle's nest.) The tree just happened to be in the middle of the golf development.

I'm sure my feelings for that eagle were entirely different from Tom's. I loved that bird! As long as he, or she, stayed in that nest, I had more time to locate a new home for Teen Challenge. God granted us more time. His favor was obvious in this situation.

In the midst of looking for property, I had the responsibility of developing new fundraisers to assist the ministry with the operations capital we needed. Not one fundraiser was consistent, and the lack of income caused me to have a difficult time meeting payroll. Sometimes the money just didn't stretch. I made sure the bills were paid, then the staff got paid, and if there were enough funds, I would get paid. On several occasions, there just was not enough income to pay all the center's bills, the staff payroll and my personal salary.

I remember the day Libby said to me, "Jerry, what are we going to do? We cannot make it without some income." We were running out of personal savings that we were using to pay our bills.

I could only go back to the hotel room where I knew I had heard the call of God in reading the book of Nehemiah. These chapters and that memory reminded me that God called me to be here and I told her, "God led us here, and He will meet our needs."

Yet, on the inside I had to battle discouragement. I felt I was not providing well for my family. My three children had no idea what we were going through, and their mother was carrying the burden for their welfare. I knew God called me to take this position and I knew I was in His will, so I just prayed it through and continued to believe God would make a way. My prayers for favor with God and man were being put to the test.

Bob Manderscheid, the board member responsible for me coming to Teen Challenge of Florida, had assured me he would send extra funds if we ran short in the beginning months, but I had too much pride to ask. My father had taught me that if you needed something, you get to work and earn the money to get it. So, I went to work. We needed a breakthrough in our ministry finances and we needed some means for generating revenue that was consistent and productive. I kept praying for favor with God and man in our finances.

Within weeks a man called and wanted to come by to talk about a project he wanted me to consider. His company kept the bathrooms clean at the Florida State Fair in Tampa; he thought we might work with him. What was the job? Keep the bathrooms clean the entire day and get paid in tips. We would have a student or two keep a restroom clean, and people could put tips in a tip box on their way out. That seemed simple enough.

But nothing is as simple as it sounds. Number one, the hours were from 11:00 a.m. until 1:00 a.m. every day for two weeks; number two, many of the people who attended the state fair went to the bathrooms to use drugs, and, number three, many of the employees who traveled with this fair were drug users and abusers themselves. So, every day for two weeks, our students, who were recovering from addictions themselves, had to clean up after people who were smoking marijuana and crack cocaine, as well as deal with the filth of the typical state fair restroom provisions.

Let me assure you that the bathrooms had never been cleaner, but we learned a valuable lesson. That fundraiser stunk! Literally! Even though we raised $15,000 in tips those two weeks, it wasn't worth the price paid in grief. Yet, as bad as it was, it provided the funds we needed to get through a tough season, and gave us time to develop new fundraising activities.

Cleaning toilets at a state fair is not a bad thing, but for Teen Challenge students who were coping with their own dependencies, it wasn't the best tool for fundraising. Nevertheless, we saw God's favor and man's favor in this event. The inopportune opportunity allowed us to think outside of the box and look elsewhere for some funding means. One such occasion came shortly after our state fair job.

In a matter of weeks, we developed a relationship with an auto auction company in Orlando. The work we did for them generated thousands of dollars a month and became just one tool we used in funding the ministry while we watched God begin to open doors of favor all over the state and nation.

Favor with God and man will become obvious as you walk out your dream. Proverbs 3:1-4 tells us: "My son, do not forget my law, but let your heart keep my commands; for length of days and long life and peace they will add to you. Let not mercy and truth forsake you; bind them around your neck, write them on the tablet of your heart, and so find favor and high esteem in the sight of God and man."

Oh, how I longed for the favor of God regarding our need for a building to house Teen Challenge. I was doing my best to stay in His Word, be faithful and trust Him. The prayer for favor became a daily prayer for me and I began to see the fruit of my faithfulness impact the ministry of Teen Challenge.

Wherever you are in your life journey, begin praying for favor with God and man, and watch God answer. Begin praying for the favor of God over your business, ministry, and family and then pray for favor with man.

Pray for favor with those you know, and those you want to know.

Pray for favor with clients, customers, vendors, land-lords, and employees.

Pray for favor with your staff, with your board, and with your family.

Pray for favor with government officials, city councils, zoning people, etc.

Pray this way and watch God give you favor, and watch people respond differently to you.

Principle 5:

STAY TRUE TO YOUR MISSION

What has God called you to do? Define it. With as few words as possible, write your mission statement and declare your purpose for existing. Keep your statement brief so you and your staff know it by heart and can quote it at any time. Then set your priorities for making the necessary moves for building your dream. Finally, plan. Evaluate your objectives and lay out your short and long term goals. To help you, invest time and money in buying and reading the great books on developing mission statements, planning and leadership. Find the strategies that best fit your mission and needs and then follow their suggestions.

Following a well-developed strategic plan is important because many distractions can steer you away from your original mission. My beginning years at Teen Challenge of Florida were at times overpowering and packed with continuous menial issues that led me away from my original focus and primary responsibilities. Not only was I required to raise the budget, but I also needed extra money for a down payment on the permanent home for Teen Challenge. Fundraising and problems great and small plagued me constantly, including staff pressures and an office chair that threw me in the floor if I leaned the wrong way. Pressure became a way of life. Managing pressure is a way of life!

One of my greatest challenges though, was the realization that not everyone enrolled in Teen Challenge should be there. One day while working in my office, I looked out the window and saw Hank driving the riding lawnmower. That may seem harmless unless you know Hank. Born with a childhood disease, Hank wore leg braces and had limited use of the right side of his body. One of my staff had given him permission to use the riding lawnmower and mow the front yard. When I looked from my window, I saw that he was driving the lawnmower in circles; he had leaned over to one side of the tractor and couldn't regain his balance. He was about to fall off. I ran to save him from killing himself. Luckily Hank didn't fall off or get run over, but I knew we had to find a more suitable home for him. Hank didn't have a drug problem, he only needed a place to stay and somehow he had ended up in Teen Challenge.

But Hank was not the only person who didn't really belong in the Teen Challenge program. We had other men who were mentally and physically challenged to the point that they could not function within the scope of our methods. These men needed help, but we were ill equipped to assist them and we were not trained to serve their needs. Unfortunately, a place like Teen Challenge can become a dumping ground for people with problems that range from being a sexual predator of minors, to being mentally retarded. Up until I came on the scene, the intake personnel had enrolled anyone in the program who was brought to the center, and I knew some boundaries and guidelines were needed to keep us true to the Teen Challenge mission.

We made a decision to rewrite our mission statement, and then stay true to our purpose: *To help youth, adults and families with life-controlling problems become established in society through faith-based mentoring, counseling, education and job training.* This mission statement became the defining framework of our ministry.

We realized we had to make the difficult decision to dismiss every student who did not fit into that purpose. We went from forty men, who had been crowded into a couple of rooms, to twenty-four men. These twenty-four men were the ones whom we could help. Hank was referred to another program.

Those beginning days were filled with events that educated me in so many situations that can happen at a ministry of our type. And one particular student taught me more than I chose to know. This student decided he wanted to make what we call jailhouse wine. He had gone out to the pasture and picked some wild mushrooms that he found under some cow patties. After letting them ferment in an old plastic bread bag, he added moldy bread and put all this in some Kool-Aid. He hid this stuff near the center in the orange grove to ferment even more. When he thought his jailhouse wine was ripe, he decided to have a party. On that night, he talked the students in his room into drinking some of his brew. The next morning, all the men who participated were vomiting and had diarrhea. Can you believe they had the audacity to blame Teen Challenge for serving them bad food? Strangely, no one else in the other dormitory was sick! After checking with the cook and finding their story had been fabricated, I began to investigate. One by one, we interviewed the students, hoping at least one of them would tell the truth. That didn't work. So we brought them all together in a circle and asked additional questions, hoping again to get to the bottom of the situation. That didn't work either. They stuck to their story—bad food—and kept blaming our kitchen for spiking their meals.

By this time my patience had run out. I told them that if they didn't tell me the truth I was going to kick them all out of the program. No one said a word, so I said, "Okay, I hate to do this, but you're all dismissed from the program. Go pack your bags." It just so happened that one student was facing ten years in prison if he did not complete the Teen Challenge program. He reviewed his options and confessed the sins of the whole group. They had drunk some of this jailhouse wine and it was the cause of the illness. He not only confessed his sins, but he ratted on the guy who made the stuff.

Needless to say, we had an interesting time that day. The student who made the concoction said, "I didn't need to confess because I had already confessed to God." He said that he was forgiven, and that he now had nothing to confess. I wasn't impressed with his theology. A donor had recently given us a new push mower, so we gave him work duty: mow the entire four acres of property. This would give him time to think about his actions. After returning to my office, I looked out the window only to witness this student start the new lawnmower, turn the power to full, lift it up and put it on a stump. Instantly the racing blade hit the stump, the shaft bent and the new mower was destroyed. Furious, I told him to pack his bags. We called his family to come pick him up.

While waiting for his family, this guy slipped out into the work shed, took some paper towels, made a fuse to the gas can in the shed, slipped it through a knothole, and lit it. A staff member just happened to see the paper burning and stopped it before it burned into the shed. When he followed the fuse, it was stuffed into the gas can. If the fire had reached the gasoline while my staff was investigating it, the explosion could have seriously injured, if not killed him. That was it: we kicked this student off the property.

His mother called the next day to chew me out for dismissing her precious son from our program. "My son told me he had confessed his sin to God, and Teen Challenge wouldn't forgive him." He had told her that we were picking on him the whole time he was in our program. She said, "You and your staff are being unfair and unchristian."

I listened, and then I asked her a few questions. "Did your son tell you that he made some jailhouse wine and got his entire room sick?"

She said, "No."

"Did he tell you that he intentionally destroyed our new lawnmower?"

She said, "No."

"Did he tell you that he tried to blow up our tool shed, and almost killed someone?"

Again, she said, "No."

"Well," I said, "your son didn't tell you everything did he?"

Again her reply was, "No."

I then asked her what she would do in my position. She said, "I would kick him out."

"Yes ma'am, you would, and that's what we've done." After she had been enlightened on all of her son's actions, she was a bit more understanding.

From this incident of jailhouse wine and similar behaviors too numerous to mention, we needed to be certain the people in our program wanted help. That's why our mission statement was so valuable. From that time on, every decision we made was filtered through our statement of purpose. This allowed us to stay on focus where we were much less likely to be distracted from our God-given goals.

Distractions, delays, and detours will always be there to deter you from your dream or mission. Stay focused; stay on track with what God has told you to do. Dreams will quickly become a reality when you keep your eye on the target. Realize that hardships are a part of the process, recognize that God is not picking on you, or making it difficult so that you will quit, but rather during the difficult times, your character and personal growth are being defined.

I have come to say it this way, "Pain is a part of the process." We have all heard "No pain, No gain." Well, my experience is that pain is a part of the process in making your dream a reality. God is not mad at you, He is not purposely making it impossible, He is just allowing you to grow through the many challenges that come to seeing a dream become a reality. That is why we want to develop our mission and stay focused.

Many needs and many challenges will get you off purpose and off mission if you allow them to. We were not a hospital for the mentally insane nor a catch-all for the sexual predators, and we had to define our purpose and stay focused to accomplish what we do well and were called to do.

Principle 6:

PLAN YOUR GROWTH

Critical to your ministry's growth is having a plan and clearly articulating it to your staff, supporters and family. Developing a strategic ministry or business plan will keep you goal oriented, and your plan will allow you to allocate resources well and create consistency between your written down mission and daily activities. A strategic ministry/business plan will not dictate all the details of your daily activities; it will not foresee every possibility; it is not set in stone, and it should not create unrealistic expectations. The plan is, however, a guide to keep you on track and focused. Your plan should be based on your ministry or business philosophy and should communicate your core values. It should consider the goals you anticipate reaching each year and should take into consideration the financial and personnel needs that will be required during the year.

Great books on planning and goal setting can better describe this foundational process and help you chart your growth. Wise leaders read and find out what other successful ministries are doing. Planned ministry growth is a must if you are to succeed in reaching your desired ministry benchmarks.

We developed a plan for relocating Teen Challenge to a property in the Orlando area. It wasn't overly detailed or well developed, but it was clear and included these objectives:

- Locate a facility that is affordable to our budget
- Locate a facility that will meet the zoning code for a residential treatment program
- Locate a facility that will accommodate a minimum of 20 men and 20 women
- Improve current program operations, training and staffing
- Develop fundraising tools; improve income and office equipment
- Create capital savings for a down payment
- Improve donor relations

These objectives look simple enough on paper, but putting them into action is challenging. After months of searching for a new home for Teen Challenge, a potential property was located, and we were able to rent a portion of the facility for the women's home. Key renovations were required before the move could take place, but the property, a church, was for sale and appeared to be a building in which we could adequately house Teen Challenge. Our plans were to rent until we could secure all the zoning and raise enough money to make the down payment.

Our first task was to remodel the small house located next to the church to accommodate twelve women. The interior of the home had to be totally remodeled. The bathroom was in shambles, the living area had to be converted into a dorm, and an office area had to be built. The church allowed us to rent an outside storage room that we needed for office space. These offices were extremely small, with six feet two inch ceilings. This posed a problem for a six foot one inch guy from Arkansas. Every time I went into my office I had to duck to avoid hitting the light fixture. It wasn't fancy, but I was happy, and I didn't have to drive to Winter Haven every day. This gave me more time to introduce the ministry of Teen Challenge to the Orlando community.

We were on our way. We had a goal, we had a vision, and we had a project. We were intent on buying and remodeling the Orange Avenue Church property into a center that would accommodate forty men and twelve women. The executive board voted to move ahead and secure the proper zoning before buying the property. The men on the executive board were faithful to do everything they could to help the ministry succeed. They gave me the room I needed to get the job done, and yet stayed close enough to let me know they cared.

A valuable lesson I have learned is that the ministry of Teen Challenge is not about locating or renovating buildings, but rather we're about developing, celebrating and building people. Teen Challenge is devoted to serving the people who find their way to our doors for help, people who are desperate in life and need answers to their addictions. Though I was preoccupied with the business of securing zoning and the business of buying a building, God was moving in the lives of our Teen Challenge students. Our planning was opening the doors to do the work God had called us to do.

We had developed a strategic plan and we stuck to it. Priorities were set and step-by-step; we met our goals, implemented our projects and kept our vision in front of us. We were growing. This is the reward of proper planning.

Principle 7:

THE CHURCH DOESN'T
OWE YOU A LIVING

No one owes you. You are responsible to work with God to fulfill your dreams, your gifting, and your chosen path in life. Whether your work is for profit or nonprofit, you have to come to terms within yourself that no one owes you anything.

This principle became a realization to me when I was working through our plan to develop an effective ministry. Many of our staff and other leaders of nonprofit ministries I had met were angry with the church. Not just any church, all churches. They felt that they were doing a labor of love for hurting people and were offended that the church wasn't doing more to help them. They seemed to have the idea that the church owed them financial support for their efforts, and I often overheard statements such as, "The church should help more," and "We deserve as much support as the foreign missionaries," and "The churches should all just automatically put us in their budget."

I soon began to realize that even though you are performing a valid, valuable ministry, the church is not obligated to support you or your nonprofit. Many worthy nonprofit organizations, most of whom are doing great works, bombard local churches with request for funding. Churches cannot support all worthwhile causes, but they often do support those ministries with whom they have established relationships. Leaders must bridge the gap between their ministry and the local churches by serving, and by providing services for them that make the relationship meaningful and beneficial for both parties.

Be willing to take the lead in building relationships. If we were going to succeed, it was up to us to begin supporting the local churches within the area. Providing beds for youth and young adults with addiction problems was not enough; we realized we needed to do tangible acts of kindnesses to express our desire to serve. We began offering our help with painting and cleaning and projects for other outreaches and ministries. We wanted people to know we were not just interested in getting their money, but truly wanted to serve the body of Christ. We have helped hundreds of churches over the years and God has blessed us with many wonderful church friends throughout the southeast. Serve them and they will support you. Love them, partner with them, and everyone wins.

Because of the nature of our work, I was very sensitive to public criticism and rejection in my early days with Teen Challenge. I wanted so badly for people to understand how important our work was in reaching those with life controlling problems. One of my chief objectives was to present quality programs when visiting churches. We worked to develop an excellent music program and trained our students so they could share their testimonies with boldness. First impressions count, and we wanted to make the most of every opportunity that God provided. We worked on good first impressions.

Early on, I realized that Teen Challenge in Florida had a public relations problem. Past failures and mistakes in leadership left many with concerns for the future of the program. I'll never forget the day I went to a minister's luncheon and a fellow minister asked, "Now, what do you do? Where do you minister?" When I told him I was the Director of Teen Challenge he said, "Oh, I'm sorry!" then immediately turned around and just walked away. Perhaps he thought I must have had nothing better to do, or maybe I was a dysfunctional preacher who only could find work at Teen Challenge. One after another I was met with similar reactions. I felt like I was fighting a losing battle.

After hearing me share my vision for Teen Challenge at this same minister's meeting, another brother replied with, "I'll give him a year. He's too qualified for Teen Challenge. He won't stay in that ministry."

On another occasion a fellow pastor asked me, "What size suit do you wear?" I told him my size and he said, "Sorry, my suits won't fit you, they'll be too long."

I said, "That's okay, the guys at Teen Challenge can use them."

I'll never forget this pastor's next statement; he quickly retorted, "I'm not giving my suits to a bunch of drug addicts." I was in shock; I knew this pastor was a great guy with a big heart and a love for missions, but I wasn't prepared for his response, and it cut me to the core. I hurt for the men that his remark affected. I hurt for the people who felt that way about the men in Teen Challenge.

A pattern of failure had been connected to the history of Teen Challenge and their reputation needed a complete overhaul. The churches were not supporting their work. I kept wondering, why, why, why? Why were so many difficulties linked to the ministry of Teen Challenge? What was it going to take to change people's attitudes? My challenge was to overcome the difficulties of those past failures, and begin new.

Money problems, moral failures, and other challenges to those in leadership had taken its toll on the credibility of the ministry. I never dreamed how much the past can impact the future effectiveness of an organization. It took two years just to begin directing people's attitudes toward change. I was met with negative responses time and time again. Thank God for that eagle! As long as it stayed nested on our old property, I had time to work on improving the public image of Teen Challenge.

Remember, the church and other ministries don't owe you anything. Refuse to allow depression, anger, or discouragement, to overwhelm you by what appears to be a lack of support from others. My experience is that you must learn this lesson, practice not being offended, and stay faithful to your call and purpose. Pray hard and work hard, and then, trust *God* to provide the support you need.

No one owes you, but developing relationships allows others the opportunity to share your passion and catch the spirit of your dream. Develop relationships. Serve those God is bringing you into relationship with. Treasure the relationships and allow God to utilize the relationships for His glory. God may not have sent droves of human supporters during those early years, but He sent that eagle! And it stayed just long enough for us to move to the next step in our incredible journey.

Principle 8:

Develop leaders around you and they will lead

The challenge of every leader, new pastor and new business owner is to build a team of staff who buy into the vision you have for the future of your organization. That is why it is so important to train and build from within the organization. Look around you right now. Who is faithful? Who is loyal? Who has a teachable spirit? What leadership gifts do you see in those around you? Do they have the capacity to grow into the leaders you need to develop your dream? What training do they need to step up to the challenge? These are the questions you need to ask yourself. When you identify those people, invest in their training either personally or through seminars and leadership training programs.

I had no choice but to develop leaders personally. Program expansion, team building and staff development were the answers to surviving and moving forward toward the dream God had given. The needs among the staff were overwhelming, and I knew that we could not take the ministry beyond the development of the staff. First, we began with planned monthly staff days. We used this time to train, build vision and eliminate "wrong" attitudes. Secondly, and the biggest challenge, was earning their trust and getting them to believe in me and in the goals I had for

Teen Challenge. Through these intentional staff days, we trained, taught them the vision, and I was able to win their respect through spending time with them and caring for their positions within Teen Challenge.

Many of the Teen Challenge staff had been indoctrinated with a poverty mentality. The attitude, "to be in poverty is to be spiritual," had integrated itself into their thought patterns. The idea that to suffer is to have been given a higher calling from God permeated their lifestyles. These crippling concepts that previous leadership had used to manipulate and control these workers' lives had to be overcome. The first order of business was to impart to them possibilities for personal and ministry growth. Some left, unable to grasp the truth that they could work for God without an attitude of suffering. Some stayed. Those who stayed began to work toward a positive future for Teen Challenge.

I knew that with proper training, attitudes could be changed. These people could be transformed into a winning, faith-filled team with vision. As their leader, it was necessary for me to model and maintain this winning attitude. Some days were difficult! Oftentimes the problems in their lives appeared insurmountable, and I despaired of any hope in changing them. But they were there, and I was their leader. I had a choice. I could either fire them all or train them all, and I chose to train them and invest in them. This was the more difficult path. You see, I had to commit to relationships with these people and spend time with them before any training would pay off.

We began building leaders through relationship building. Our monthly staff days became a time for sharing and training. The format was simple; we would open with worship and prayer, follow with testimonies and then share what God was doing in our lives and in the program. This was always an exciting occasion for the staff as they disclosed stories of new students, who were coming to Christ and being set free from drugs.

Next, I would teach on basic principles of leadership. Many had never heard these principles discussed, but they were eager to acquire the knowledge that would help them advance in their personal lives, as well as learn individual leadership skills to help them with their jobs. This training was the right action at the right time. From this process, we weeded out those who would not allow themselves to change or grow, thus structuring a foundational team eager and willing to make a difference. As in Jim Collin's book, *Good to Great*, he said, "It is important to get the wrong people off the bus and the right ones on the bus, and then, work to get them into the right place on the bus."

The core group was now ready to advance. More extensive training and relationship building was the next step. We planned a staff retreat, three days of time together away from the base, working on team building. Here I wanted to begin identifying those with leadership potential.

One of our board members graciously offered his Captiva Island beach house to us. This house was designed in such a way that it was great for retreats and large group meetings. God must have smiled at the astonished faces of the staff when we stopped in front of that multi-million dollar home. That poverty mentality was to be challenged over the next few days.

I wanted our staff to have a great time, and I wanted them to see that I knew how to relax and have fun. So I rented a couple of wave runners for the afternoon, had a ski boat available, and took time for some R&R. They couldn't believe that I would spend money for them just to have fun, but I knew it was important to play together as well as work and pray together.

I reflect on that first staff retreat with fond memories — staff members falling off wave runners and struggling to get back on, everyone laughing as they watched the crazy antics of Bobby Curry, racing over the waves like a psychopath, with me on back hanging on for dear life. Once he flipped me into the ocean, leaving me at the mercy of the waves, and didn't even realize I was treading water. I screamed for him to come back, pleaded with God to protect me and finally resolved to lie there until he realized he was without passenger and decided I deserved to be rescued. Everyone on the shore was laughing and yelling at him to get me.

And something important happened that day — we began to feel like a family. When we gathered to share God's Word and share vision, the staff began to see my commitment to them, and to Teen Challenge. They realized I felt they were worth the investment of my time and our money. My dedication to them worked, and we were on our way to becoming a team.

Our staff training and parties have only intensified as the years have gone on. We now invite leaders who are running similar programs to come and join us for staff getaways. Over the years, hundreds of visitors have benefited from just being a part of the dynamic of that day. Our staff days are packed with an unlimited energy, and I have never encountered such a feeling of belonging. We really enjoy our times together. We work hard, but we also play hard.

And that has made all the difference in staff unity, performance and attitude. We're a team!

We now conduct Teen Challenge Directors' Retreats for three or four days every October. Together, seeking God for His direction, we use this time to outline our plans for the upcoming year. We work for a portion of the day, we pray for a portion of the day, and we play for a portion of the day. Whether golfing on the greens, sunning on the beach, or shopping 'til they drop, the leaders take this opportunity to cultivate one-on-one relationships with one another.

In addition to our annual October retreats, we plan an April trip to work on subsequent skills. Again, we concentrate on the essential, but we also kick back and have fun together. God has supernaturally provided housing with no cost to Teen Challenge for all of our trips, and we have stayed in some breathtaking estates: Hilton Head, Fripp Island, Sanibel Island, Captiva Island and Mission Inn are to name a few. We give God the glory and we know that our praying for His and man's favor has paid off when we share in such luxuries and abundance.

These training days have allowed me to develop leaders who now run our ministry. We staff several directors who went through the program, worked their way up the leadership levels and now serve as directors. What a joy it is to experience how they now expand the ministry by, in turn, developing the leaders around them.

Having the right leaders makes it possible for me to do my job. The best investment we can make is in our greatest asset, our staff. Building a strong staff provides the freedom I need to upgrade other programs, pilot my leaders, establish donors, and have time for planning. Your current staff is your greatest resource for selecting leaders in your organization. They are already acquainted with your work, with your product, and know more about the heart of your organization than anyone from the outside. Develop the leaders around you! Take the time to teach them. Take the time to know them. Feel their passions; hear their concerns; listen to their suggestions; learn from them! Maintain your role as the leader, and remember team leadership is the most effective leadership!

Principle 9:

LEARN TO LAUGH

Laughter does good like a medicine. And during my first months at Teen Challenge, I had to learn to laugh and look at the lighter side of so many unbelievable issues. Facing one crazy problem after another, I had to learn to take life's realities less seriously and realize that even though circumstances might be bad, they could always be worse or get worse.

We worked hard; we planned; we dreamed and we pushed ahead, but at times, the mountains facing us seemed overwhelming, and we didn't know which direction to take. Learn to laugh at impossible situations, and then, put your trust in the Lord, knowing that He can handle anything!

During my first year of leadership with Teen Challenge, I had to make several staff changes, which caused other staff to live in fear. There was an attitude of resistance to change, which made every decision more difficult than it should have been. Some staff left because they couldn't believe in, and follow the vision, and others left because they didn't have faith to believe Teen Challenge could be any better than it was.

Some weeks there was little money, many problems, and what felt like a million things that needed done. Repeatedly, I returned to Nehemiah four, "Restore the walls with those burned-over stones." And burned over they were! But there was beauty for ashes, and amazing works happened in those early days. One of my fondest memories is sitting in my little storage room office praying a simple prayer, "God, please give us favor with You, and give us favor with man." And He did. Day by day, challenge-by-challenge, we went to work, traveling thousands of miles, speaking in hundreds of churches, and sharing the ministry and vision of Teen Challenge. I logged 94,000 miles on my little Nova during the first two years, and thousands more on the Teen Challenge vans.

One Sunday evening around eleven p.m., tired, and glad to be back at the Winter Haven Center, we returned home from a full day of ministering in church services. When the lights shown on the front of the center, we were speechless. What we saw was unbelievable. A herd of wild hogs had camped out and lay snorting and nudging on the steps and porch of our center! When we got out of the van, the pigs scattered everywhere. We were in shock. Wild hogs everywhere, running all directions. I didn't know what to think, but evidently, the students were thinking, "pork chops." Within days they had captured most of those pigs. We decided to keep some of them fenced up, and raise them for food. The students, becoming somewhat too attached to one of the largest barnyard swine, named her Pork Chop.

The day came when Pork Chop was to be offered up as pork chops. Tim, one of our staff members, was to do the dirty deed. Pork Chop stood about four feet tall, was about six feet long, and must have weighed seven hundred pounds or more. Tim borrowed a rifle and prepared to finish off old Pork Chop. Taking aim, he shot! But just as the shot rang out, Pork Chop moved. The bullet hit her in the snout. She squealed, jumped and ran right through the fence, full steam ahead through the orange groves. Tim was chasing her, shot after shot, trying to put her out of her misery. Finally succeeding in taking care of that business, it was time for the next step, getting Pork Chop cleaned and dressed out.

Tim and a couple of the students got a truck to drag old Pork Chop under a tree, planning to hoist her and skin her. Using a rope, they tied her up, then threw the rope up over a large oak branch. The other end of the rope was tied to the bumper of the truck. Starting the motor, they began to pull her up. The tree limb began to bend down and the rope stretched tight. Before they got her up to the acceptable height for skinning her, the rope broke. They got a second rope and started the process over again. The tree branch bent, the rope tightened. Snap, another rope gone.

Now, we all know that difficult jobs call for serious minded people, and it was time to get serious. Tim and his merry men got a chain and put it over the branch, connected it to the bumper of the truck, and began to pull her up. As you might expect, the branch broke! They threw the chain over a bigger limb and began again. This time it looked like everything was working, she was halfway up off the ground when the truck tires began spinning.

I watched as the tires disappeared, buried in the sand. Amazing! I laughed until I cried. But these men never gave up. Leaving the truck stuck, they took shovels and dug an enormous hole under Pork Chop. Finally they could clean her.

Let me tell you, pork chops were a treat at Teen Challenge. Stories circled constantly describing lean times: bread and butter diet for days at a time; French onion soup donated by an exclusive restaurant, sounds good enough on the surface, but when you have it three times a day for two weeks, the taste for it dims, exclusive or not. Another time, a student assigned to work in the kitchen opened a fifty-pound bag of rice, only to find it full of bugs. The cook, knowing they had nothing else to serve, said, "Don't worry, those bugs won't hurt anyone. It looks like wild rice and a little extra protein tonight." The students ate it and no one said a word. Stories of eating wildebeest and shark were shared with lots of laughter.

Perhaps the worst story of all described a night when there was absolutely nothing to serve the students. The cook marched out to the remains of an old swimming pool, took a couple of turtles out of the six or seven inches of water that was well hidden under a coat of fungus, and sacrificed them for soup. I can't verify this tale, but I do know things were tight for a while, and we had to believe God for everything.

After I had been there just a couple of weeks, a man drove up to the center with a truckload of lemons and limes. He brought them believing he was being a blessing. The problem was that more than half of them were rotten—covered with mold and slime. Out of ignorance, I took them and said thanks. It took our students days to dig enough good lemons and limes out of the pile to make a few gallons of limeade, and I realized we had done the students a disservice.

The gift wasn't worth the time and effort it took to get the value. The next time this fellow showed up, I told him no thanks, we didn't need any, but I appreciated his thinking of us. He took offense, said I was being ungrateful, and promised never to bring us any more lemons. I felt badly offending the gentleman, for we are thankful for what God provides. But I have learned that every gift is not always a gift. We have spent enough money getting rid of junk dropped off at the centers to know when to say no. I can't tell you how many console TV's and worn out lazy boy chairs we have had to turn down or throw away. We even have good Christian folk wait until we all go to church, and then, they bring their throwaways and leave at our front door. A great challenge for any nonprofit leader is being able to refuse gifts offered by people who want to help, but do not understand the time and effort it takes to dispose of unusable products.

Even as these daily opportunities to laugh at ourselves increased, the challenges of rebuilding the walls continued. Patience and diligence were my virtues, and I often felt a kindred spirit toward the words Nehemiah had written, "There was so much rubble to be moved that we could never get it done ourselves." Only the spirit of the Lord could guide us through all the rubble.

Many pastors and individuals over the years had been disappointed with Teen Challenge of Florida; I felt compelled to work toward healing those relationships. I remember meeting with a pastor of a great missions-giving church, hoping to win his support. But he had been hurt by Teen Challenge leaders in the past and wanted nothing to do with me or with Teen Challenge. He said simply, "Prove your vision. We only send you $25.00 a month because a lady in the church designates it for you. We won't help you with your vision until you prove yourself."

During the three-and-a-half-hour drive back to Orlando from this luncheon, I argued with God. "Why did you bring me here to fail? Why do I have to live down the past? Why do I have to live down someone else's mistakes? Why are so many holding bad attitudes about Teen Challenge?"

Warm tears of self-pity and frustration flowed that day; I felt so alone in my efforts and passionately sorry for myself. I was hurting from rejection; and I was taking it personally. I was upset with God for moving me to Florida. But the truth of the matter was this: This pastor had given thousands of dollars of support for a local Teen Challenge center in the past, and the money had not been used by the Teen Challenge state leadership as the church had designated. The center eventually closed down in that community, and this pastor had a right to be protective of how he spent the funds his congregation donated.

On another occasion, I visited a local church to introduce myself. The pastor was a young man, on assignment in his first pastoral job. My purpose was to get to know him and share my vision for Teen Challenge. His secretary was rude, literally treating me as though I were a street beggar. Even though I had an appointment, due to a counseling session that ran overtime, I waited an hour and a half. I was nice and just waited. Finally, his office door opened, and he exited with an attractive young lady. He told me he was sorry, but he had to run. He said he didn't have time now to see me. "Just leave some literature," he told me.

Arrogant and pompous, he acted as though he were God's gift to the church. I must confess, I began to get angry. But, remembering I was trying to get the church behind Teen Challenge, I held my temper. I left the office, got stuck in five o'clock traffic and was an hour late getting home. Who did this guy think he was? How could he be so insensitive? The whole hour I griped and complained to God, often times wiping the tears of rejection from my eyes.

"Why is it so difficult?" I kept asking myself. Then I would go back to Nehemiah for direction. The Lord spoke to me time after time from Nehemiah four. I knew these experiences were the result of the walls being torn down at Teen Challenge, just as they were in Nehemiah's situation. These were great days and horrible days all at the same time. Understand me; I knew I was in God's will, but God's will is sometimes a difficult place to be. I look back today and laugh at some of those crazy times, but then it was not so easy to laugh.

The students who were coming into our centers at that time were precious to me. All kinds of people, from all walks of life were entering Teen Challenge for help. We had a former Golden Glove boxer who was headed to the Olympics, a former tailback for the Green Bay Packers, a former executive with Winn Dixie, medical professionals, chefs, street bums, general laborers, teachers, and many more. Gifted, and not so gifted, the common thread that drove them all was the need for this ministry.

One of the students who especially stands out in my memory is a veterinarian who came to Teen Challenge for help with his drug problems. He had become addicted to horse tranquilizers, better known as PCP. Enduring a rough childhood, John's dad was an alcoholic who beat on him whenever he was drinking. As this was the case more often than not, John spent less and less time at home and began sneaking into a veterinarian's clinic after hours to have a place to sleep. Eventually, John made friends with the veterinarian who owned the clinic and gave him a job. He gave him keys to the building, and set up a bed in the backroom so he would have a place to sleep. Through his association with the doctor and his connection with the animals, John grew to love his work and developed a passion for the veterinarian practice.

John attended college and earned a doctorate degree in veterinarian medicine, but the pressures of business got to him and he began using the drugs that eventually destroyed him. On the verge of losing everything, John was ordered to go through the Teen Challenge program or lose his license to practice medicine. Not long after coming to the center, John gave his heart to Christ and Christ gave him the peace he had been looking for. Praise God! He called me one day about a year after he had graduated to say thanks. One student after another being set free from drugs and making Christ Lord made all the challenges worth it all.

You see, even in the midst of challenges, we were still making momentum. We were still reaching lives, we were still working on finding a new home for Teen Challenge, we were still focused on what God had called us to do, and there was fruit from our labor.

We were on track even though the road was rough. Rough roads are no excuse to get off track. Stay in the fight and keep your momentum and you will eventually see the reality of your dream. When you get things moving in the right direction, keep moving. Do not sit down or you may stop the momentum. It is so much easier to get things done when you have momentum.

What I want you to realize is this: There will always be opposition and challenges to your vision. Find the humor in some of the circumstances and laugh. Look for the positive. The fruit of what you are trying to do is there and coming into reality. So, don't give up before the miracle. Give yourself a break; laugh a little, cry a little, relax, and enjoy the journey.

Principle 10:

OPPOSITION IS A PART OF
THE PROCESS

Accepting opposition is a part of the building process for any nonprofit. Challenges will come in all shapes and forms and adversity will strike from the least expected sources. Dead ends, refusals and setbacks will happen. And I have only three words of advice for when it does: "Deal with it." Anyone who has ever tried to build a ministry has had to face opposition, but remember the cliché, "Anything that is worth having is worth fighting for." And fighting is exactly the way I felt as I searched to locate a home for Teen Challenge. I never dreamed how difficult it would be, and I never anticipated the numerous problems we'd face with staff and students.

One of the most challenging periods and one that tried my faith and tested my understanding was when we were finalizing the negotiations for the purchase of the Orange Avenue Church of God property. For months, we had spent hundreds of hours working on funding, planning and developing the property into a possible center. We had spent thousands of dollars securing our variances for handicap codes and our zoning approval; and we had pulled every dollar we could find in order to propose our bid on the property.

When the day came for negotiating the purchase price with their church board, my Board of Directors and I had stretched our faith and offered our best bid, which we felt, a fair offer. But previously, the church's realtor had estimated what we felt to be an inflated value for the church property. A couple of the board members felt they wanted to hold out for what the realtor had suggested. They refused our offer. They said, "No." I was astounded! I was crushed! We had prayed fervently; we had worked diligently. We had given our best offer and it was not good enough. "No!" That was one of the hardest "no's" I've ever had to accept.

What followed was a series of "Why, Lord, why's: Why after hundreds of hours in prayer and planning? Why after scraping together all the money? What is Your purpose in this? Why, Lord, why? W—h—-y? W———h——y?" All of which led me to another one-on-one conversation with God Himself and another trip to the book of Nehemiah. And what I found encouraged me. At least for the time being.

Within the course of ridicule and insult, threat and frustration, the Israelites led by Nehemiah worked with all their heart, closed the gaps, prayed to God and shouted, "Our God will fight for us!" I stepped back, planted my feet, breathed in deeply and bravely accepted the loss, "Okay, Lord, I'll let You do it Your way."

The search for new property was on. My exploration (under the direction of the Lord) led me to thirty or more different buildings, none of which suited our needs. I looked at an old hospital vandalized and lying in ruin. Apparently, several homeless had sought its shelter as the stench of human waste and urine was everywhere. The structure was beyond renovation. I remember asking God, "Is this all you can afford for Teen Challenge?" We visited an old vacated church that had bats nesting in the arching ceilings of the main sanctuary. Bat droppings were in piles all over the platform, pews and flooring. We held our breath and removed ourselves as quickly as we could reach the exit.

Again, I asked God if this were all He could afford and if this were all He had for Teen Challenge — buildings filled with human and animal wastes. Not long afterward, I became depressed with the process. I was sick of looking at buildings that were either too far gone for repair or those we could not afford. My hopes were dashed time and time again. Nothing fit our need. Nothing fit our budget.

Desperate for a Location

Three months later, we located a bankrupt retirement home in Ft. Lauderdale. The location was not what we wanted; but, we were getting desperate and I thought maybe we could place the program there temporarily while we kept looking in the Orlando area. This facility, in horrible condition, however, housed thirty rooms each with its own bathroom, a commercial kitchen, a lounge, a sitting area and three fenced-in acres. We knew with a great deal of hard work we could transform this dump into a suitable center. One advantage was the fact that its location was in an area laden with prostitutes and drug addicts. The opportunities could be endless. We offered a bid of $150,000 to The California Federal Bank. They accepted; we paid $15,000 down and began working on zoning.

Upon suggestion from a local counsel, we set up a meeting with the community to discuss our interest and future plans for our newly purchased facility. Previously, I had met with a local neighborhood pastor and a few of the church folk who were behind us, and they generously offered their church building for our meeting. We invited the residents to attend an informal gathering to discuss the Teen Challenge Ministry and our intentions in their community. To our surprise, a massive number of residents came to this meeting and were ready to fight. Armed with anger, rage and vice, they attacked us with vile and hate-filled comments. We were addressed as their worst enemies; and even though they were well aware of the current use of the building as a home for transients and drug addicts, they would rather have it remain in that current state than have a Teen Challenge program move in.

I was even accused of being a racist because my family and I personally were not moving into the area. We had a local director who was in place to direct this center. They didn't understand and neither could I convince them, that I, as the state director with headquarters in Orlando, just couldn't move there! But no reasoning settled down this mob-like crowd. They were determined for us to stay away or make our life miserable.

Later, I found out that the city had pushed a couple of other housing projects on them without their input, and they were upset. They took all their aggression out on us. They were not upset with Teen Challenge or me personally; they were just afraid and unable to see beyond their fears. At that point, I knew we had to look for another building.

The meeting did not end until 10:00 p.m. and we had a three and a half hour trip ahead of us. Hundreds of thoughts sped through my mind as we began the drive to Orlando, including thoughts of my speaking engagement scheduled for the next morning. My mind raced. My daughter, Deneé who was eleven at the time, went with me that night to keep me company. After we got into the car, she looked up at me and asked, "Daddy, why were those people so mad at you? Why did they say all those mean things?"

I tried to explain it to her without appearing negative. She was quiet for a moment and then said, "Daddy, I don't think I'd like your job very much."

I continued the drive, feeling so desperate, so rejected, so confused as to what God was doing. What was I doing wrong? What now? Where would we go? As I thought about what Deneé had said, I realized I wasn't sure if I liked my job very much either. Once again, I asked, "Why, God? What are You saying? What do You want me to do?" What a soul searching drive that was. Had I missed the call of God on my life?

Once more, we had lost several thousands of dollars and hundreds of hours of work. The quest for another building began, again. We found buildings, many buildings; some too expensive, some too big and others too small. We found buildings, some with wrong floor plans, some with poor design, others with bad zoning. We found buildings, lots of buildings, buildings with all kinds of issues.

Then one day unexpectedly, my realtor called and said, "Jerry, it's a long shot, but you might be interested in an office complex that is in bankruptcy." She went on to say it was developed at a cost of several million dollars and had 35,000 square feet of space. The facility had five acres of land with 185 parking spots. It had landscaped walkways, air-conditioning units in each room, fiber optic phone lines, skylights, good carpet, ceiling fans, office space, dorm space and virtually everything we needed except a commercial kitchen and showers. Yet again, I got excited and began work to make an offer only to find that Seminole County was also interested in buying the building. After a brief time, the sellers informed us that they were only going to consider the county's interest.

Do Know This — It Can Get Worse . . .

To top things off, back in Winter Haven where our men's home existed, lightning struck the tree where the eagle nested and the tree burned to the ground. The eagle moved and the next day the developer, deciding to construct a golf course and modular buildings on the land, began knocking down every big tree on his entire four hundred acres.

Within days, bulldozers had pushed down every large tree, including thousands of orange trees and were burning them. The developer called, "Jerry, I can give you sixty, maybe ninety days. Then we'll need to push the houses down where the men live. You've got to move." I could not believe what I was hearing. A year and a half of hard work and nothing to show for our efforts. How could so many things go wrong in one ministry? Where was I going wrong?

In addition to finding a Teen Challenge facility and facing the soon evacuation of Winter Haven, my wife and I needed to buy a home for our family or be obligated to pay profit gains taxes on the sale of our last home. Presently, we were renting a home and had looked at what I would say to be hundreds of houses while my wife would say it was only a few. I had no idea where the new Teen Challenge Center would be located, so we found a home close to the interstate, one we deemed would work, and we decided we would go ahead and buy. The home was suited for my family needs, and I could get on the interstate quickly and drive wherever I needed. I didn't realize it at the time, but that decision was one of the best I would make.

Next on my agenda was our staff retreat, but a retreat was the last thing I wanted to plan! Constantly my staff was asking where we were going, what we were going to do and if we had a center yet. Some staff feared the loss of their job and sent out resumes for other employment. That really boosted my faith! In the midst of the constant questions and a job-searching staff, the dirt piled up around the house. Daily, the bulldozers dug up trees, pushed dirt and served as a constant reminder to everyone that we needed to move quickly. Not only did we deal with the dirt, but also the dozers broke our water lines, left us without water for several days and then dug up parts of the septic system. Due to the constant earsplitting roar of the dozers, class time was challenging, discussions were intermittent and thinking was impaired. And the staff were frustrated with no idea of our future.

The timing couldn't have been worse for our annual staff get away. Here we were with sixty days before we were to move out, and we had no place to go. What was I going to tell the staff? How were we going to have a meaningful staff retreat with these issues facing us? Teen Challenge was in trouble and I was still the leader. My desperation rose to new levels. I knew I had heard from God, yet

I felt so alone. I knew we had to press on. So, I planned the retreat.

Room to Grow

On the first morning of the retreat, I went running on the beach and as I cooled down and walked back toward the beach house, I sat down, looked out across the gulf and began wondering what I was going to do. Again, I asked God the same questions He had heard me ask so many times before. "God, what now? What do I do? What do you want me to do?"

Hurting desperately, I had absolutely no clue what to do. Knowing I was at the end of my rope, I told God, with a bit of an attitude, "As I see it, we have forty students and staff, all kinds of stuff to move, people depending on me and no place to go! Why did you bring me here to die, Lord? All I know is I have done all I know to do! I need Your help! I need Your direction!"

With tears in my eyes, I just sat on the beach and waited. I waited on the Lord and He showed up and I listened. His still small voice spoke to me, and I knew the Lord had heard my cries on the beach that day. Clearly, I heard His direction," Read about Isaac's wells."

I thought to myself, "Isaac's wells, what's that got to do with what I'm experiencing?" I remembered preaching a sermon once about Isaac's wells, but it just didn't seem relative to this situation.

But as I continued to listen, I sensed the Lord saying, "Read the scripture about Isaac's wells." I didn't remember where the story of the wells was located, but I went inside and promptly searched my concordance and looked up the story in Genesis chapter twenty-six. The story unfolds as follows.

Isaac and his people were living in the land of the Philistines. Because of Isaac's prosperity, which during the Old Testament times signified power, the Philistines asked him to move away from them. Isaac did what the Philistines asked him to do and he uprooted all of his family and all of his belongings and moved into the desert area of the Valley of Gerar. There he dug a well and found a fresh supply of water, but the shepherds of Gerar became jealous, and they, too, asked that Isaac move on. Isaac agreed but before he did so, he named the well *Esek*, which meant "strife."

Once again he uprooted his people and journeyed deeper into the desert. For the second time, he dug a well and once more the shepherds of Gerar became jealous and stirred up strife. So Isaac named this well *Sitnah*, which meant, "continued strife." Isaac moved again and dug another well; but there was no quarreling there, so he named the well *Rehoboth*, which meant "God has given us room to spread out, and we will prosper in the land." I began to ponder these thoughts and words, and the Lord began to speak to me.

The Lord shared that the first well, *Esek*, named strife, represented the Orange Avenue Church of God building. The value of the property was in dispute. We had tried to settle on land in an area of strife and that was not the place God chose for us. We had to move on. Then God went on to explain that the second well, named *Sitnah* or continued strife was symbolic of the Ft.

Lauderdale property where the community rose up against us; and although a great investment of time, money and labor had been spent, this was not the home God wanted for Teen Challenge. The community never would have supported our cause, and the strife would have been continual. We had to move on. And finally, when Isaac dug the third well, *Rehoboth*, God's promise to be with Isaac and bless him became reality. The Lord spoke to me and said that He had a *Rehoboth* for Teen Challenge, a property with room to spread out and one that would prosper. He told me to trust Him.

Faith leaped up in me! I knew the Lord was with me! I knew He had a *Rehoboth* for Teen Challenge! Suddenly, I had confidence that God had everything under control. Did I have a building? In the flesh, no, but in the Spirit, yes. My heart beat rapidly as I reflected over the parallel of Isaac's wells and the past two years of my life. Being responsible for the devotions that morning, I shared Genesis 26 with my staff. I told them that I had heard from the Lord and that I was confident that all was favorable. They rejoiced with me and their hearts filled with faith. We sat in unity, in one spirit, refreshed, reenergized and ready to watch God's next move!

The Lord taught me great lessons during this time of immense opposition. I had no idea what our next step would be. I had no Plan B, but I did know this:

- God called me to walk through Nehemiah 4
- God wanted to restore the broken walls
- God walked me through Genesis 26
- God wanted me to locate in the Orlando area
- God promised He would provide the *Rehoboth*.

God had taken me to the point of total dependence on Him. Now, I just had to wait. I had to wait on Him. And during this time of anticipation, I encouraged my staff to:

1. Pray hard
2. Work hard
3. And pray God will bless your work.

I am a strong advocate of prayer. I believe that your dream, vision or special project will not work unless you bathe it in prayer. But I also believe that since the beginning of time, God decided to put legs on man in order for him to walk out the vision. Therefore, secondly, God won't do through a miracle what you can do yourself through hard work. Working smart is key. Many people work to the point of exhaustion, but they don't get very far. You must stay alert to God's Spirit and stay open to new ideas and ways of doing things in order to save time, money and effort. Then you are working smart! Finally, you must pray that God blesses the work, or all of it may be done in vain. You must cover the project in prayer, or you, rather than God, may begin to rule and drive the project. Once God is no longer in the driver's seat, the leader is in the danger zone. You must remember that it is not through our might or even the gifting that God has given us but through God's Spirit that your project has succeeded.

During that two years, God refined me, refined my vision, refined my faith and proved me. I completely surrendered to the Lord, and I was prepared for whatever lay ahead no matter how difficult. Dr. Paul Cho, famous pastor and author, claims, "Never trust a man who doesn't walk with a limp." I had been broken and I was limping. But God used our opposition to steer us to the miracle He had for us. The adversity was part of the process that had to be experienced for God to direct us where He wanted us. What lessons we learned! We had a miracle around the corner, and the opposition we were facing was driving us to the very spot God had in mind all the time.

Principle 11:

LEAN INTO GOD'S PROMISE

In the heat of the battle, when challenges are many, lean into what God has promised. Keep a moving forward posture. Lean into the call. Lean into the opportunity before you. Trust your instincts and the passion in your heart for the dream God has given. It is so easy to lose your focus in the face of so many challenges. Events, oppositions, fallen-through deals, and even people, can get you off track and sideline your purpose. Circumstances may call for the redefining of your dream, but if you stay focused on the goals, your hard work will pay off quicker. You will be able to better filter your options, and the desired results will hit the target.

One pitfall to leaning in to the promise God has given is comparing yourself to others. Looking at how other non-profits or businesses are doing and evaluating your success against your cohorts can lead to frustrations and an inaccurate measuring system. God's plan for your ministry is unique, delegated by God, designed by God, developed by you through God. Copying a fellow worker's plan is not the direction you need to cultivate yours. Even though we can learn unlimited lessons and utilize a few ideas from here and there, your God-called ministry is individualistic in purpose and intent. Keep the focus on your call and lean into the promises of God.

After returning home from our staff retreat, I felt

focused and confident. I had a promise from God, "I have a Rehoboth for Teen Challenge." I knew God had everything under control; however, I knew we needed property and needed it ASAP. Two days later, my realtor called me about the property in Sanford. She said, "Seminole County has decided not to follow through with their plans to purchase the Cardinal Industry properties. The building is available. Are you still interested?" I tried to remain "cool." I didn't want to appear too excited for fear that they might run up the price. I expressed my interest, and we agreed to meet at the property for a walk through. Both the listing agent and my realtor came for this tour and as we got out of the car, the agent warned, "I hear there are snakes out here and that the snakes have multiplied since the company went bankrupt and the property has been abandoned."

Now, please understand. I hate snakes. I hate all snakes and snakes unnerve me. I have never met a snake I liked, and this day was not going to be the exception. As we entered the main entrance, I shared a remark about the snakes, I said "Oh, don't worry. It's daytime. We'll see them if they are out. They won't bother us."

We began checking out the first building. As we walked room to room and from building to building, I was filled with anticipation. I visualized what might work in each building and each room, and I was very overcome with all the space. The possibility seemed too good to be true that this facility might actually house our new Teen Challenge Headquarters.

And then it happened! As we were leaving the second building that we had toured, I opened one of the exterior building doors and stepped out, as I did a three-foot rat snake fell from the above door frame where he had been napping. In one quick movement, I opened the door, and this green slimy snake landed on the back of my neck. The two realtors following me through the door, screamed and ran back into the building. I felt the snake on my neck. Was life over? Was I to die at our future site? I slapped at my neck. I jumped up and down. I screamed! I slapped at my neck again! I rebuked the devil and spouted out the scriptures "that we can tread on serpents." The problem was I couldn't tread on him because he had gotten stuck on my collar on the back of my neck! I played out the scene. My contorted antics to remove my predator had failed! Visions of the cold-blooded viper biting me on the neck came flashing through my mind. Flashbacks of stalking cobras in the jungles of India and illustrative excerpts from the movie *Anaconda* overshadowed me. Finally, my drama was interrupted when I realized the snake was gone and had fallen to the floor.

I stood trembling. "What just happened?" I realized I had just had a snake on my neck. I also realized that with great force, the door had been slammed on my way out of the building and the snake had met his destiny. Smashed to death in the door. Justice was served! The Lord's vengeance was mine. I had smashed the life out of him!

Concerned for the welfare of my fellow tour companions, I looked around to see that they had run to the end of the hall and were laughing uncontrollably. Even though visibly shaken, they finally came through the door. And after they were convinced of my well-being, we all again began to laugh. We laughed so hard, but humor was not going to prohibit keen senses and acute alertness. With definitive caution, I opened each remaining door determined to never again be necklaced by a sleeping rat eater.

Thirty-two thousand square feet! This property had 32,000 square feet of floor space, offices, air-conditioning units, vaulted ceilings, large asphalt parking lots, ceiling fans, restrooms, a conference room, beautiful landscaping and much more. I just could not imagine how we would ever fill it.

Then, we approached the last building. I reached for the doorknob only to find it very difficult to turn. As I shook it and pulled it and pushed it and shook it again, I realized I was in trouble. From the corner of my eye, I saw the flying formation swarming toward me. I looked up to see the huge wasp nest that I had disturbed. For the second time, the realtors screamed and ran.

This time, I joined them. I thought as I began to make my way off the porch, "All I need to do is outrun these two realtors in heels and I'll be safe." But it was too late. Stung once. Stung twice! And then a third time which kicked me into high gear. I outran the realtors and lunged to safety. Neither of them was stung, and although I was hurting, I couldn't help but laugh. And even though the realtors joined in with laughter, they felt sorry for me at the same time. We finished the rest of the tour without incident – for which I thank God! I wanted this property and I wasn't about to let the devil run me off with a serpent and a few locusts!

All Blessings Flow

I called my board of directors and invited them to view the property. I wondered if I should buy reptile repellent and a can of Raid, but it wasn't necessary. They shared in my excitement and agreed that the property would make a great site for Teen Challenge. Nations Bank, now Bank of America, accepted our offer of $440,000 to purchase the buildings. We were now officially under contract with plans for the property to serve as the new Teen Challenge of Florida Headquarters! This facility was large enough to accommodate our men's home from Winter Haven and the women's home from Orlando. God gave us a multi-million dollar property for only $440,000! As the Psalmist says, "Praise God from whom all blessings flow!" And we had been blessed! As an additional bonus for me, the center was only eight miles from my recently purchased home! I kept the focus on our need and God honored us in the process!

Despite the fact that we were excited and knew we had received our *Rehoboth,* the time was one of tremendous pressure. We had just ninety days to get the proper zoning, secure level one and level two environmental audits, arrange termite and roof inspections and the list goes on. The pressure to meet deadlines was apparent, and we desperately required additional finances. We had paid the $25,000 down which we had raised during the past two years. The contract we presented stated that in ninety days we would pay an additional $125,000 to close on the loan and complete the deal. Again, we sought a miracle, but remember, I believe "you never get a miracle until you need one." Well, we needed one and it came!

During this same time, we had been asked to vacate the Winter Haven facility within sixty days. The developer was in the process of constructing a golf course and modular homes and wanted the building we were leasing out of his way. But it would take ninety or more days before we could even be assured that our new property would receive the zoning change for which we had applied. Then and only then could we begin the renovations, which would take a minimum of three months. Needless to say, my faith was stretched. We lacked furniture for the offices and dorms; we had no equipment for the commercial kitchen, no washers, dryers, lounge furniture and just about anything else you could think of, we didn't have. Rooms required remodeling. And we needed to add twenty-two showers, fifteen toilets, fifteen sinks, design and construct the commercial kitchen and complete the laundry facilities. Whew!!

For everything to come together, we were expecting several miracles. I went to the Word and to Nehemiah 4 to learn what Nehemiah had done when rebuilding the walls. During that time, God often spoke to me, and I focused my attention and energy on listening to His direction. For the next three months, my staff and I worked sixteen to twenty hour days. We prepared for the city commission and zoning meetings. We obtained layout architectural drawings and worked on floor plans. We took care of environmental audits and required inspections. I wrote hundreds of appeal letters for financial support and asked for volunteer workers. God opened the door to what was the greatest series of blessings that Teen Challenge of Florida had ever seen. But the principles I mentioned earlier were in full force. We prayed hard. We worked hard and smart. We asked God to bless our work. And we did all in turbo speed!

As a result of our focus and our persistence, we reaped the following series of miracles:

- Due to some holdups, the developer allowed our men's center to stay in Winter Haven longer than we had anticipated.
- A generous donor gave a $50,000 gift toward the new facility.
- Bank of America donated 6 twenty-four foot truckloads of office furniture, valued at $100,000. We counted 119 office arm chairs, cabinets, safes, wall pictures, a conference table and more.
- Bank of America donated a stainless steel commercial serving line and numerous items for the kitchen.
- A donor from Tennessee gave us a twenty-four foot stainless steel hood, serving line, and kitchen utensils.
- Cash contributions purchased all the other equipment for the commercial kitchen.
- We received the zoning permit we needed.
- We received the needed loan from The Bank at Winter Park.
- We were given a thirty-extension phone system.
- We raised an additional $75,000 from other individual gifts.
- "Speed the Light," an Assemblies of God Youth Program, donated a new fifteen passenger van.
- China Coast Restaurant donated storage shelving for the kitchen.
- Sea World donated tile for the kitchen.
- A pawnshop donated wallpaper, yard mainte-

nance equipment, and tools for the garage.

We closed on the loan and God presented *Rehoboth*!

A Home with Room to Grow

The payments on the new facility were actually less than the total of all the properties we had been renting. And now, we owned our property. What a blessing! As an added blessing, I now had an office where I didn't have to duck when I walked in, one that had vaulted ceilings, air conditioning, and my own bathroom ——wow! God had wonderfully supplied!

Eagerly, we began the remodeling work on the student housing, chapel, kitchen, dining hall and classrooms. The project would take another four months of sixteen – twenty hour days. The "ox in the ditch" principle from the Bible was in order, and we needed to get it out. So, the extra work and effort on all of us was what it took to get the job done. Everyone worked as they had in Nehemiah 4, hand in hand and in one spirit. Alan Bullock headed up the remodeling project while Tim Newborn kept the men's home in Winter Haven operating. A crew of students who had construction background were recruited to assist with the labor. We moved them into one of the buildings and set up a temporary home for them. We turned a wash closet into a shower and installed a temporary kitchen to get us by until the commercial kitchen was completed. What a challenge!

Believing that the area communities and churches would share our zeal, I had anticipated other ministries and local organizations getting behind us and providing teams of volunteers to assist us on a regular basis. I mailed letters, made phone calls, and yet, it seemed that everyone was previously committed to other projects or just didn't want to become involved. Then, I realized we had "a lot" of work to do to heal the past feelings that many were still holding against Teen Challenge.

We didn't focus on sleeping snakes! We didn't focus on swarming bugs! We didn't focus on the lack of community support. We kept our focus on our vision! We focused on the property, on prayer, on funding, and on manpower. We focused on the hundreds of lives that were going to be turned around! We focused on God! The result—our new Teen Challenge State Headquarters!

Principle 12:

YOU CAN FUND YOUR VISION

No money, no ministry! Bottom line. If you don't already know this, you'll learn it soon enough! First and foremost to the success of your ministry is realizing that funding your vision is just as spiritual as any other part of the vision. The biggest challenge is your attitude about raising funds. You don't have to be afraid of fundraising, you just have to be sure your attitude is such that you don't resent it or avoid it.

Secondly, realize that raising support and developing an income through some creative means is critical to your dream. We were able to utilize service contracts in our adult programs, utilizing student labor for support of our ministry. Thirdly, develop a funding plan/calendar that will assist you during slow periods of giving.

The responsibility of vision support can often be overwhelming and is an area many would choose to avoid; however, it comes with the turf, and God expects us to step up to this challenge, meet our obligations—and at the same time—assist other ministries.

Principle Number 2 states, "Pray hard. Work hard. Then pray God blesses your work." Praying keeps us humble, close to Him and able to hear God's directions and suggestions for productive and creative fundraising. I so often have found myself in prayer over finances only to watch God's hand go to work. Next, do your part. Brainstorm with your staff, followers and friends. Read the books on how other nonprofit organizations fund themselves; search the net for info, e-books and free software; and seek the advice of those who have previously organized nonprofit businesses similar to yours.

God tells us in Proverbs to make plans by seeking advice. Keeping an open mind and a willingness to learn from others is a strategic step for continual money flow. Pray that God blesses the work you do, and remember that He will overlook our lack of perfection.

With the anticipated growth in both student enrollment and staffing increase, we recognized the need for new means to bring additional funding into the ministry and to accommodate the growth of our programs and the recently purchased facility. Along with believing God for His divine provision and implementing our faith, we also asked Him for imaginative fundraising ideas.

One of the values we teach in developing positive lifestyles is to uphold a good work ethic, and I realized that one of our greatest assets was labor. Even though our students performed daily chores, which included the care and maintenance of the facility and grounds, and some assisted in keeping the vehicles in good working order, they were not learning occupational skills for their future careers. I believed we could better advance their talents by providing job training opportunities and at the same time teach them self-sufficiency skills by allowing them to assume a portion of their cost at Teen Challenge. Therefore, both the students' needs and the financial need of Teen Challenge could be served.

Knowing that we had the manpower that many companies in the Orlando area looked for, we teamed with an auto detailing business in central Florida and with an Orlando auto auction company. Both provided many of our students with on the job training plus salary. Several of our graduates have continued to work for the auction company or have gone on to start their own auto detailing businesses. In this situation, we utilized labor not only as a teaching tool but also as a method for fundraising.

Fundraising is a basic responsibility for developing your nonprofit ministry. And during the support process (which is usually ongoing), you will find that the key to fundraising is building relationships—relationships with the churches you serve, relationships with the people you serve. Notice the word *serve*; serving is key to developing any relationship. Work to develop good relationships with everyone you meet and surround yourself with those who have influence and affluence toward your cause. Do business with those you hope will partner with your vision. In turn, these relationships may provide opportunity for monetary and provisional backing and when one asks, "How can I help you?" these words have opened the door for you to honestly share your vision and wish list. In one situation, we approached some boat owners to donate their boats to Teen Challenge rather than sell them. We received more than twenty boats. We cleaned, polished then sold these boats and used the proceeds to support the program.

Believe God — Then Go to Work

Generating new revenue maximizes your ability to move on. I once heard someone say, "When God guides He provides." And another said, "Money follows ministry." I agree with these sayings, but someone else said, "There ain't no free lunch!" God guides and He provides, but I have yet to see ravens drop off cash at Teen Challenge. Pray — spend time in prayer and on your face before God. Believe God for your provision. Then, go to work. Develop creative means to raise support and avoid listening to the one who says, "We've never done it that way before." Brainstorm with your staff. Brainstorm with your Board of Directors, your contributors and your friends. And remember there are all kinds of ways to raise money.

Our next challenge was obtaining funding for the remodeling of our new facility. And we had no other choice but to find new ways of generating revenue. Remodeling the facility was crucial to our opening, and it demanded that our staff and students work endless hours repairing and redesigning the 32,000 square feet of space. We needed a place to house our men as soon as possible, so we decided to permit each one to live separately in each of the seven buildings. This would enable us to begin moving students into the buildings as they were completed. Our hard work paid off. Within three months of purchasing the facility, we moved our men's center out of Winter Haven and the women from Orlando into the Sanford property. The monies we needed for renovations came, and the Lord continued to provide as we did our work.

As your vision grows, the need for additional funding grows. Growth costs, and this is an issue every nonprofit faces. When I was in my first pastorate, I felt my first year's goals were to love God, love people, and preach the Word. That was it. That's all I felt I needed to focus on. Then, God began to bless the church with growth. In the beginning, it seemed that the newcomers were all people in need and even though they were good folks, many appeared to call for assistance themselves and were unable to give to the church. Our budget was stretched and stressed and I asked God what to do. I felt a clear sense of Him saying, "You minister to these and I'll send others who can support." And that is exactly what happened. Our church grew and the Lord added many additional families who contributed time, energy and finances.

When your finances are challenged, look to God for direction. God has promised us "exceedingly, abundantly more" and if finances are tight and challenging, there is likely to be a reason. First, break down your accounting methods. Closely calculate the outflow of monies. Be sure you're spending appropriately. Be sure the bills are paid. And if you are not good with money management, find someone who is. God will honor us if we are wise stewards with our money and gifts. You have a responsibility to assure that you or others are not being wasteful.

Secondly, as a leader, examine yourself and your staff. Ask God if there is unconfessed sin or mistakes that may have stopped the flow of the Lord's blessings. See if there is any "sin in the camp." Remember the story in the Old Testament where Achan took those possessions (the devoted things) God had told him not to touch. (Joshua 7:20-21, NIV) The entire nation paid for his sin. After searching your own heart, encourage your staff to do the same and to seek the righteousness that draws God's favor.

Finally, make certain you are supporting the needy and are giving to other ministries and missions. God instructs us to give to the poor and expects us to share our blessings with others.

Faithfulness: The Price of Your Dreams

NOTE: There is an ebb and flow with finances; it just seems to be a part of the process. And although "balancing the checkbook" may seem impossible at times, God rewards the faithful. Repeatedly, he has rewarded us by meeting our needs just in the nick of time. Remain faithful. I encourage you to stick it out even when it's tough and it appears you're the only one who cares. It's your dream, and the price of your dream becoming reality is faithfulness. The return for your faithfulness will come. For me, it was watching some of our most desperate students turn to Christ at Teen Challenge. We now had the place and the programs to help them. God met our need. He provided our *Rehoboth*.

As the project neared completion, a new student, Randy, enrolled in our program. His story was one of the saddest I had heard. When he was seven, Randy's drug addicted mom kicked him and his five-year-old sister out of the house and told them never to come back. Randy shared, "I remember digging through garbage cans for food. I always gave the best I found to my sister. The police eventually picked us up and put us in foster care. I never saw my sister again and had no idea how to find her. When I was twelve, I tracked down my mom and paid her a visit. I rang the doorbell; she opened the door and just stared at me. I said, 'It's me, Randy, your son.' She slapped me, and cursed me out, pushed me off the porch and told me to never come to her door again."

Randy was crushed and couldn't understand how his mother could feel this way about him. He wondered what he had done to make her hate him so and reflected on his last memories of being around her, searching for the answers to his questions. He never found them. This rejection caused Randy to develop a hatred for women. He abused most of the women he became involved with, developed drug and alcohol dependencies and was indescribably taken advantage of by a 35-year-old woman. By the age of twenty-one, Randy was destroying his life.

Randy had never been given the chance to succeed. Knowing only pain, heartache and disappointment, in extreme depression, he came to Teen Challenge. Randy was filled with so much internal anger that he struggled greatly in getting along with others. In fact, before he shared his story, we almost dismissed him from the program.

He was difficult to deal with and was always making someone angry. Then the day came when Randy responded to an altar call and gave his heart to Jesus. Gradually, he began to make the changes necessary in dealing with his past, and through his healing, he has become a living example of God's willingness to change the worst of circumstances. Thank God for his ability to change a guy like Randy. All the extra effort, all the hours, all the stress, and challenges were worth it!

We were being faithful and worked hard at the financial aspect of our vision. We sought every means of fundraising we could think of and carefully considered every proposal suggested on how to raise money. The following is a list of the various fundraisers we have utilized over the years:

- Holding an annual banquet
- Fundraising luncheons

- Walk-a-thon, Bowl-a-thon & Jog-a-thons
- Golf marathons and tournament
- Garage sales
- Cleaning churches and businesses
- Washing cars
- Building and selling computers
- Catering services
- Silent auctions
- Sponsor-a-student campaigns
- Monthly donors
- Monthly newsletters
- Washing airplanes
- Doing yard work
- Painting businesses
- Operating a thrift store
- Hosting a pancake breakfast
- Working a candy project
- Working at Honey Baked Hams during holidays
- Selling donated land and houses
- Selling donated boats and cars
- And, of course, we wrote hundreds of grants.

No money; no ministry!! It's as simple as that! It's as complicated as that! No fundraiser is ever too small nor too massive. Pray hard. Work hard. Wait and watch God move the mountains of money problems and bless your world with "exceedingly abundantly more" than you ever dreamed possible! You will find what works for you, and over time, you will get more and more comfortable with the ebb and flow of funding your vision.

Principle 13:

Keep your family in focus

Leaders under God's call to develop their ministry sometimes without intent neglect their families, and I was no exception. Non-stop projects demanded 16-20 hour days for months on end. I was spending less and less time with my family and more and more time doing "the work of the Lord." This is the trap that you must watch for. Some time passed before I realized my crimes of neglect and the trap that I had fallen into, a trap that could eventually cost me my family and one that certainly kept me absent from many memorable moments. I had witnessed many ministers' families destroyed due to the lack of the husband's presence, and now, I was plunging into the same deception. God revealed the error of my ways; I repented, refocused on my wife and children; and God's gift of grace enclosed me.

However, before my "truth time," two and a half years passed by. I was exhausted and worn out, yet excited. We loved our new home; we loved Rehoboth, and often when I walked the grounds, tears of gratitude filled my eyes. I reflected on our challenges, those times of emptiness, doubt and faith, faith and doubt and those "nick in time" miracles the Lord mastered. The experiences had been more than I ever expected.

During the day, I donned my white-collar attire, raised money and ran the ministry. During the evening, I lost the tie, changed into work clothes and helped with the remodeling. Eight months—eighteen-hour days. Rarely was I home before 2:00 A.M. and Libby, my wife, often brought my dinner to the center so she and the children could see me. And even though Libby, raised on the mission field, understood sacrifice, she had reached her limit. The lack of my presence combined with her resuming all responsibility for running the household and handling family pressures had surged beyond her level of tolerance.

Family Matters More

The "straw that broke the camel's back" was a mouse! Libby can handle spiders; she can deal with snakes, but a mouse is a different critter and when mice invaded the privacy of our garage, that was the straw. The scampering little pests took residence in my boxes of stored books and shortly after building nests, thereby increasing their enrollment, plotted migration into our kitchen. Hospitality toward these creatures was not in her plan and now Libby demanded action. And that action was to be administered by me! I was to alter my work habits, eradicate the mice, "Mr. Clean" the garage and adopt a new library for my books. After successful implementation of my "rid a mouse plan," we realized we needed a break! We needed a vacation! And we needed one yesterday!

Graciously, my family and the staff were offered the use of a wonderful place on Captiva Island, Florida, for three weeks. My family, eager for the getaway, shopped, planned, packed and repacked. Visions of reclining in a lounge chair, sipping on fresh lemonade, and soaking up the warm rays while listening to the rocking of the waves heightened my expectation of the "so needed break." I would relax, fish from the pier, relax some more and enjoy the laughter of our children as they played and constructed high-rise "sandominiums." All would be good. Or so I thought. And then, my Hallmark sketches transfixed into a sad rendition of *National Lampoon's Vacation*. Relaxation was a thought and nothing more.

My "Type A conquer the world" personality had refused me the privilege of vacation and for the first week, I had integrated training sessions into the activities and entertainment for our staff. In simple words, a well-needed rest by all was reshaped into a job. No relaxation. Not even "fun" work. Just work, and I was relieved when the week was over. "Now," I thought, "We'll have a great time. Now, I will get out of the fast lane. Now, I will watch my day-dreams evolve into the Kodak moments." But again, I missed it. I could not relax and exerting effort to try was exerting in itself. I could not sit still. I had to be doing something. I had to be doing something. I had to be doing something.

After the second week, Libby loaded up the children and left. I knew that I had not been good company and that she most likely was glad to get away from me and back to her work commitments. Before she left, she said, "You need some time alone so you can get back on track." And she left and I was alone for a week–all alone — no appointments — no deadlines — no zoning issues — all alone, just me, a big house and a beach. Plenty of time to live out my original visions of relaxation. I walked the beach, I jogged. I prayed. I read. I just listened. I would sleep for hours during the day, awaken to read a little more and then return to sleep. I was exhausted, burnt out, and I needed hours upon hours of rejuvenation. The project was finished. The big push was over and the high was gone. I was refreshed, rested and ready to go back to work. It was now time as Libby said, "to get back on track," to relax and resume a realistic pace, and to be a husband and father again. And as I sought rest, balance, and renewed strength, "something" was still not quite right.

I returned home determined to live and work a more controlled schedule. I enjoyed the new facility and my work in the ministry, but again that "something" that was not quite right overshadowed me. Even though my physical and ministry lives were more controlled, my emotions were unusually sensitive. I would find my eyes filling with tears when hearing certain songs on the radio, and becoming blurry eyed when viewing billboards that triggered certain responses. Being one who does not cry easily, I soon realized my emotional reactions were acute.

My assumptions were further verified when I shared my experiences with a friend, Dr. Jimmy Lee. Lee had traveled to Florida from Chattanooga to conduct a Turning Point seminar and while riding with him, I began to share my experiences. After carefully listening, he said, "Jerry, you are suffering some light depression." At first, my response was disbelief and denial. What? Me? No way! Depression? I am a man of faith, a guy who just led our ministry into a massive campaign in securing a multi-million dollar facility! Not me! Not depression. I wasn't giving up the fight that easy. I had nothing to be depressed about. Then reality landed.

Yes, me. Yes, depression. My inability to relax, my project-driven tendencies, my need for constant challenge, and my inaccuracy in securing solid family relationships had totaled into an emotional draining and void that opened the gate for the slow growing opponent of depression to slip in. From that day on, Jimmy helped me identify my feelings and helped me put "some things" in perspective. It took over a year for me to get myself "back on the right track." Many days were trying and difficult. During the process, I had to renegotiate my relationship with Libby and my kids. I committed every Tuesday to date night with my wife. I arranged for babysitting and made the plans for the evening. I purposed taking days off and spending quality time with my kids. With the help of God and friends, I won my family back. I won my life back.

Don't Push the Oxen into the Ditch!

Jesus illustrated the parable of the ox in the ditch on the Sabbath to teach his disciples. I began to use this parable with a "Jerry twist" as an excuse with Libby that the ox was in the ditch and we needed to get it out. This analogy allowed me to resort back to my driven methods, work countless hours and justify it as doing God's work. I soon learned that there were many oxen in the ditch and that there seemed to always be another ox, another project. New opportunities arose daily and I found myself slipping again into a trap. My wife, wise beyond her years, caught on to the over-uses of this strategy and pointed out to me, "Jerry, you are pushing oxen into the ditch." She went on to explain that I was project-driven and that I needed to slow down. She was right. Not only did I not fool Libby, but one of my board members also identified my vices and shared, "The Lord guides and the devil drives." He, too, was telling me to slow down. They were right. And since then, I have worked on learning how to pace myself a little better.

God is about people. God is about family. God is about relationship. Your family matters more than the work you do, even if that work is 100% ministry.

Companionship and communication are essential to building healthy relationships and both require the giving of your time. When companionship and communication are absent, the door has been left open for the husband or wife to seek relationship at the office, at the church meeting, or from whoever will take time out and listen to them. If you don't have the time to communicate with them, they will find someone who will. Sadly to say, the family may face the danger of break-up. Your ministry, vision and dreams must include your family and must always be second to your spouse's needs. Take the time to kill the mouse. Build the "sandominiums" with your kids. And don't push the ox into the ditch!

Principle 14:

EXPECT GOD TO EXPAND YOUR ORIGINAL VISION

Throughout my spiritual journey, I have come to realize that God generally gives me just enough information to take one step at a time. He has never made known to me the entire plan during our first prayer time or revealed all the steps of the growth process at the beginning. I get a "Yes, go ahead" and I step out in faith or I get a "No, not now" and I stop or I get a "Wait" and I pause until I get "Proceed." During the unfolding of my dream, I have found that God always expands the original thought or vision to something much broader than I could have imagined. He expects me to be faithful, move on His direction; while along the way, He blesses me and provides added opportunities. Amazingly, this principle always works. One step at a time, one day at a time, and the process evolves; the vision enlarges, and God sheds more light on what has been His strategy all along.

Locating a permanent home for Teen Challenge and settling my family into a new area were what the Lord was calling me to do. But while traveling the State of Florida, preaching and sharing the vision of Teen Challenge, I began to get a burden to open additional centers in other Florida cities. Within the state, I visited city after city with enormous populations, with enormous addiction problems and with no Teen Challenge centers.

The state's drug czar, Jim McDonough, released fig-
ures indicating that there were (at that time) over eight
hundred thousand identified alcohol and drug abusers in
Florida. The need for providing more centers and the need
to expand my vision was apparent. And with sixty percent
of all illegal drugs entering the United States through the
Florida borders, we knew we had a significant problem and
that we were only scratching the surface of the demand.
God was expanding the vision.

We were receiving between one hundred and four
hundred calls monthly from moms and dads desperately
wanting to place their child in our programs. My heart
broke having to say no to so many hurting parents. Often
the beds were full and we had to put them on a waiting list.
On one account, a young man on our list died in a car acci-
dent with a friend who was drinking. If we had possessed
an available bed when his mom called, that boy might still
be alive. I knew we had to provide more beds.

I first considered our women's crisis center in Ft.
Lauderdale to establish if there was room to expand our
services in their facility. We had been using the property as
a referral center for men and women who sought placement in our programs around the country. At the same
time, the Salvation Army had given us the use of a duplex
rent-free; so, I decided to convert the duplex into a
women's residential center. We would be able to accommodate eight women, we opened the doors and God began
to send us those who were seeking help with their dependencies.

Inside a couple of weeks of opening the program in
Ft. Lauderdale, Phil, a graduate of the Winter Haven men's

center, called me desiring to open a Teen Challenge facility in Ft. Myers. Phil had graduated the program some years earlier and had gone on to obtain an education, but now, with a burden on his heart, he wanted my permission to position his family in the Ft. Myers area, get a job and begin raising interest within the community for Teen Challenge. With my blessings, Phil set up a phone line to answer calls from those needing help with their addictions, and it wasn't long before the phone began to ring with parents calling begging us to help their children. God provided us an opportunity and we bought a home to open the men's home in Ft Myers.

We were growing. We wanted to be faithful to God, but we also did not want to get into a financial pinch. The Sanford men's center continued to expand; the women's home in Ft. Lauderdale was full, and now we desperately required bed space in Ft. Myers. God was expanding our vision, and at that moment, we had to wait for His next move.

His next move came delivered in the form of a letter. During the spring of 1993, I was opening my mail and read a note from a dear lady who had seen our newsletter and thought we might be interested in some land she was willing to donate. I went to visit her and found out that the property not only included a home, but also forty acres of land. Ten of those acres were covered with Valencia orange trees. The property seemed ideal and after a couple of visits, she decided to donate the home and all the acreage to Teen Challenge. I was so excited to know that God had heard our cry and that He was providing the means to transform our dreams into reality.

We remodeled the home to accommodate our program, cleaned up the property and moved in some students. We worked hard to develop a center at this location, but it was so far out that it was very difficult for our students to acquire jobs. In time, it became clear that the wisest option was to sell this land and invest the proceeds in a better location. The property sold for $115,000 and we placed this money into savings so at a later time we could draw on it for the right purpose.

During the summer of 1993, my staff and I, needing a time of refreshing and training, attended the National Teen Challenge Conference in Washington D.C. I remember sitting in a session with many of the directors and staff from around the country, listening as director after director spoke on how desperate they were for staff. Their programs were suffering for lack of trained personnel. God began to speak to me and showed me that some of the space at our Sanford center could be converted into a staff training school. Now all we needed was the curriculum and a leader.

Paul Palser, my father-in-law, a former missionary and pastor of forty years, was visiting one summer and felt God speaking to him about moving to Florida and assisting me. Paul resigned his church, sold his house, packed up his belongings and moved to Florida. The first four months of his time were devoted to developing curriculum. Courses he could not find, he wrote. Both he and my mother-in-law worked endless hours researching various resources in order to secure the best text and to write the finest instructional programs for the school.

We opened the following January. The school filled up quickly with men and women hungry to learn and be trained for leadership. We have now had the privilege of placing graduates all over the United States and around the world to work in Teen Challenge centers.

The Vision Keeps Expanding

As we were getting the Ministry Institute up and running, the Lord opened another door for our consideration. Doug Wever, an employee for National Teen Challenge was visiting Florida for the purpose of doing an onsite accreditation inspection of our facilities. As we traveled to our current centers, Doug mentioned his burden for the Daytona Beach area. He asked me if he were able to raise his support if I would consider hiring him. We prayed and decided that if the funds were raised, we would move forward. And within just a few months, donors had taken on the challenge, and we were ready to hire a full-time director.

We joined forces with another ministry who was renting space from the Holy Trinity by the Sea Episcopal Church and began working with the runaway kids on Daytona Beach. *Time* magazine reports that there are more than five hundred thousand runaways that our government considers "throwaways." These kids live on the streets of America and have no homes. Many of them find their way to Daytona to attend the MTV beach concerts. The number of runaways overwhelmed us, and we knew we needed a residential home for those requiring placement.

We witnessed to so many young girls passing through that we came to realize that we had to open a juvenile girls home. There were too many kids with no place to go. These kids were desperate, with no hope and a great desire to be loved. One day I was at the runaway program, and I noticed a group of four girls who were obviously prostituting themselves. One of the girls sat down on a couch, so I decided to sit beside her and ask her a couple of questions. After I asked her name and where she was from, I then asked how it was that she had come to be in Daytona. She explained that she had run away from her home and wanted to attend the MTV concerts on the beach. I asked why she felt she had to run away.

She looked at me and began her story. She said, "My step-father would come into my room at night, any time he wanted, and molest me. My mom knew what was going on but wouldn't do anything about it. She thinks that she can't make it financially without him, so she let him do whatever he wanted. I hate him."

She went on to explain, "I used to take a butcher knife to bed with me and ask God for the courage to kill him. He would get on top of me and I wanted to stab him. But I never could, so I ran away."

I'll never forget the next words she said to me. She looked me directly in the eyes and asked me, "Mister, would you go home to that?"

I replied, "No." When I said, "No," I knew I had obligated myself to try and help her and hundreds like her. If I couldn't send her home, where could I send her? I believed we needed to provide her a home, give her a chance, provide her with an education, and love her as God did.

My staff and I prayed and believed God to help us find a home. In answer to our prayer, I got a call from a donor who had a large three-story home for sale in Deland. The donor let us know that if we could use it, they would sell at a very reasonable price. So we made an offer, worked out the contract and bought the home. We opened the home for twelve girls and the beds filled up immediately.

God continued to expand our vision, and we were experiencing the blessings of watching Him work within the hearts of countless who were alone and without expectation.

The Episcopal Church that we had leased space from for our runaway program began looking to relocate and decided to sell their building. The priest who was leading the church at that time had a real love and appreciation for Teen Challenge and offered us the first option to purchase the property. After praying, he wanted us to have the church and wanted to make it as cost effective as possible. They quoted us a very reasonable $290,000, and although it would be a real challenge to our budget, the local advisory board and the executive board were of the opinion that it would be a wonderful opportunity for expanding our outreach in the Daytona area. I had no idea how we would pay for this building.

One day, a local businessman who had a specific interest in our runaway program came by to see our work. I walked him upstairs to the area where some of the runaway youth were congregating and something amazing happened. He spotted one of the youth who had been hit in the eye with a baseball bat. This young boy's eye was unbelievably swollen and several shades of purple and his cheek was laced with several stitches. He really looked terrible. The man asked me if he could pray with the boy, and I told him yes, if the boy would allow him. Slowly, he approached the boy and asked if he could pray for him. The boy looked at him, hesitated but then agreed. Placing his arms around the young man, he began to pray aloud. The other youth in the room stopped what they were doing, became very quiet and listened as he prayed. When he concluded, he hugged the boy, walked over to me and with tears filling his eyes exclaimed, "I'm going to help you buy this building." Realizing that the emotion of the moment was very strong, I was hoping his words would manifest very soon, and then, just a few days later, he wrote us a check for $50,000.

Due to the number of runaways and the number of those who could easily be taken advantage of, the pedophile and child molestation problems are overpowering in Daytona. We believe God has called upon us to reach them and present them with a means of escape. These youth are primarily from broken homes where they get very little, if any, parenting. Some eighty-five percent of the girls who have run away are being sexually abused at home by a parent, stepparent, relative or neighbor. Their ages range from twelve to eighteen years with the majority being between fifteen and sixteen, and at times, we have had as many as two hundred different youth come by our home within a month. We minister to them. We feed them. We clothe them. We get them clean. We counsel and encourage them, and when we can, we send them home.

At that time, we had four operational centers equipped for men, women, runaways, and juvenile girls. I was content to stay and stabilize these centers, but God had more in store.

Our men's home in Ft. Myers continued to grow. Greg Hammond became the director and under his leadership, we built a duplex (debt free, thanks to a generous contributor) purchased another nine houses (all of which are debt free) next to us and we now have bed space for forty-eight men and twenty-two women. God continues to expand the program. Families are being reached and put back together. Mothers come knocking at our doors asking us to help their husbands or children who are addicted to drugs or alcohol. Many are touched; many are blessed. And so are we!

Not long after the completion of the project in Ft. Myers, God touched a dear elderly lady's heart during one of our church services and she wrote us a check for $25,150.00. Although an unusual amount, I did not hesitate to accept it gladly. When I called her to thank her for her generous gift, she shared that she had fifteen acres she wanted to donate to us for a new center. I drove over to Tarpon Springs to view the property and discovered some of the most beautiful land I have ever seen. The grounds were lined with hundreds of live oaks and from the property front, you could see three gated communities with homes valued at $350,000 and up. So when she offered this gift, we felt that God was clearly opening the door for us to establish a center there. We accepted the gift and then had the property appraised. The land was worth approximately $485,000. God had a master plan for that property and for us, and now, it had become a reality. God keeps expanding our vision.

We thought that we would have difficulty obtaining the proper zoning in that area because of the surrounding neighborhoods. However, God loves eighty-eighty-year-old ladies and by a remarkable miracle, no one showed up at the meeting to contest our desire to build a Teen Challenge facility in that location. Having sat through numerous zoning commission meetings and listening to irate citizens threaten words like "we are going to burn you out" makes you a little nervous. But apparently, God had a different plan and His timing was perfect! Several miracles began to manifest for the funding to construct this building.

As I was about to leave on a fundraising trip to Tampa for our Tarpon Springs project, I stopped by my home and asked Dustin and my wife, Libby, to pray. I told them, "We need a miracle. We need $250,000 to get this project finished. Would you guys pray with me and ask God for a miracle?" We prayed and I headed for Tampa.

Mark Romano, the local director, and I went from business to business asking them to consider "gifts-in-kind" contributions for our building project. We met with electric companies, plumbing contractors, roofing companies, supply companies and everyone else we could think of who were willing to meet with us.

A plumbing business agreed to do all the plumbing for free – some $32,000 worth of supplies and labor. An electrical company helped secure virtually all of the electrical materials and provided the labor at little cost and the friends of Teen Challenge within the area gave generous donations toward the project. Within a three-day period, God supplied $135,000 in "gifts-in-kind" contributions and $100,000 in cash gifts. Other donors pledged their support. God touched the Tampa Bay community, and they reached out and helped us; and now, we have a beautiful twenty-eight-bed center with a new commercial-equipped kitchen, staff apartments and completed offices.

Heading West

As we were completing the Tarpon Springs project, one of our advisory board members offered us property in the Tallahassee area. I knew she had a heart for the ministry, and she had forty acres she was considering donating. The donation of the property never came to pass but as a result, I began investigating the possibility of opening a center in Tallahassee or the west Florida area.

An existing ministry in Bonifay that had closed down its operation approached me. The Circle H Ranch had a hundred acres of land, a three-bedroom home and a residential facility that would accommodate about thirty students. But due to under-funding, they were unable to maintain and had not been able to raise the necessary finances to keep the program operational and were about six months behind on all their bills. The Circle H board wanted Teen Challenge to consider taking it over and opening it as a Teen Challenge ministry. We prayed, believed God had opened the door, and we bought the ranch and started the renovation process.

We decided to use the facility for a boy's center. Enough monies were raised to build the new offices, classrooms, and staff apartments debt free, and we had space for one hundred students. God had provided us with a ranch complete with a fancy bunkhouse, plenty of country air and several barnyard critters!

Black angus cattle, goats, and other farm animals wandered our grounds. We felt the country setting was exactly what many of our students needed, and when working with a hundred youth and adults, even a hundred acres can become small. We have since purchased 50 more acres of land with four chicken houses and a five thousand square foot house and are building a thirty five thousand square foot student life building.

This facility has seen hundreds of boys lives changed in this beautiful country setting. Richard was one such student.

Richard came to Bonifay to get help for his drug dependency. Drug abuse had stripped Richard of everything he valued in his life. He had lost his family, his home and all else that was dear to him. He had never been on a farm and didn't have the slightest idea about raising or caring for cattle. While walking the pasture one day, he ran upon a newborn baby calf. The mother had abandoned it for an unknown reason and without nurturing, it would die. Richard's heart went out to this little calf and since he didn't want to see it die, he asked what he could do to save it. He began to bottle feed the calf and it wasn't long before the little calf would follow Richard all over the ranch. Wherever Richard went, the calf went. The moment Richard came out of the house, the calf would come running. The calf would bump Richard in his posterior as Richard walked, indicating that it wanted some milk. As Richard continued to care for the abandoned animal, his heart crossed the threshold for healing. God had given us this ranch to get guys out of the city and allow them a chance for a simpler life and a fresh start.

Shortly after we had completed the renovations of the Bonifay ranch, the West Florida District of the Assemblies of God offered to give us a church in Pensacola. Even though the church had closed down, the District wanted to see it utilized. They told us, "If you will open a Teen Challenge in Pensacola, we will give you the property plus

$5,500 the church has in savings." On the down side, the structure called for unlimited renovations in order to accommodate twenty residents; but on the up side, it already was properly zoned for a residential center.

Renovations began. We had to install an $11,000 septic system, fire safety equipment, a commercial hood, a suppression system and the list continues. After $50,000 of improvements, we were all set to open. Soon more than fifty students were participating in the program. We eventually out grew this facility and purchased 83 acres with fifty-five thousand square feet of dorms, commercial kitchen, chapel, hotel type dorms and have watched the program expand to more than 115 men. Under the direction of Allan and Gwen Vann Horn, the program in Pensacola continues to explode. A new women's home is underway.

BACK TO FT. LAUDERDALE

For four years we had searched for property to purchase for our women's program in Ft. Lauderdale. We continued operations in rented facilities, but the staff had hoped and prayed for their own place. On one occasion, we attempted to buy a nursing home, but the deal fell through. Then we located a home in Davie and put in a bid, contingent upon zoning. The home would have been excellent, but it was one hundred feet too close to a current adult living facility. We asked for special exemption from the zoning board and we were voted down. The results — five votes against us and zero votes for our exemption. The city council members claimed, "We like what you are doing but find a property that fits the city code and we will be happy to have you in Davie."

The directors, Ricky and Donna Fernandez, were becoming depressed. Every other Teen Challenge center in Florida had their own facilities, and yet, they had been with the ministry the longest but had no residential center of their own. We could not understand why God was not opening the doors for them to locate a facility for their own. Eventually, our realtor located another home in the town of Davie that met the city code, and we were able to secure the building permits in writing before we began the remodeling process. We raised $100,000 for the down payment and we borrowed the remainder. We spent $75,000 for both the renovations and the meeting of the city code. Miraculously, all the monies for the remodeling and the labor were donated.

The series of events that followed were shocking and challenging. During the last week of remodeling, a couple of ladies in the community decided they didn't want us in their neighborhood. Because of their insistence, the Mayor of the Town of Davie called a town hall meeting to permit the citizens to voice their concerns. The problem was that these ladies had gone door to door and spread rumors that were inaccurate in their descriptions of Teen Challenge. Those attending the meeting were more like a mob than a gathering of concerned citizens.

The city attorney and zoning staff began to describe how we had met the current codes and that we were already permitted in this zoning. The crowd grew angry and began shouting and threatening us. Calming them was impossible. Convincing them our students would not hurt their children or steal their cars was beyond impossible.

The man I referred to earlier, promised "to burn us out." I was shocked; we had met all our legal obligations and we had obtained the zoning license and permit in advance of purchasing the property.

A week later when we went to apply for our occupational license, we were refused. The city said that these ladies had filed an administration appeal and that we could not move in. The politics took over and the city's position changed, and they decided that we could not inhabit the property. We had paid $200,000 for the home; we had spent $75,000 in renovation to meet the city code for a group home and now they were saying we could not use it. We had no choice. We were forced to file suit against the Town of Davie.

God Comes Through

The Federal Fair Housing Act allowed us to place six students in the home while we proceeded with the suit. We rented another site for our women which created some challenging issues since we operated in two locations but had to utilize the same number of staff. Our expenses doubled and we faced the expense of the lawsuit. Our Ft. Lauderdale project took three years of patience and more depositions than I care to remember. But again, God came through. We won the case. We won the right to use our facility as permitted and we won the $30,000 plus for attorney fees. And if that were not an accomplishment in itself, the city of Davie had to pay us for all the rental expenses of the second home, all our travel expenses to and from the second home and more.

Praise God! We didn't gloat in the victory, but we did

shout loud and clear that our God reigns. Sixteen ladies plus staff now live in the home and since our opening, we have built a student life center for the purposes of fellowship, chapel services and family visits. Beautifully landscaped with a small pond and some live-in mallard ducks, our place has become a haven for healing for so many women struggling with life-controlling problems.

Tremendous Growth in Florida

In the course of a few years, Teen Challenge of Florida has developed centers all across the state. This development process grew into the opening of an average of two new centers each year for seven years. A committed staff along with donated miracle properties, land, supplies and tools transformed our dreams into a reality. By the end of 1999, we went from having a capability of housing forty students in a rented facility to owning fourteen centers with the capacity of accommodating four hundred. God's hand was on us and we were thankful. His plan for expansion has taken us on an unknown journey—a journey of expectation, a journey of faith, a journey of disappointment, a journey of restoration, but most of all, on a journey of knowing that we are in His will and are working His plan. And that plan was traveled one step at a time, and He blessed us and expanded our territory.

Principle 15:

USE CONFLICT TO YOUR ADVANTAGE

Life is packed with conflict and when doing the work of God or establishing your own business, you can expect a measure of conflict. Conflict happens to everyone and is a part of life. Demanding people, difficult financial crises, a few lawsuits, leaks in the roof, family issues are to name a few. On the other hand, conflict, while a challenging part of life, can be transformed into our advantage and actually work for us.

When addressing conflict, the first step is to get your attitude in check. Examine your attitudes. Are you angry with God because of conflict in your life? Do you feel you're purposely being punished when it seems everyone around you is prospering? These attitudes must be brought to prayer and dealt with. We must realize that God is not the enemy. He cares about you, is for you and not against you and desires to see you prosper in every good thing!

Secondly, conflict can often clarify direction. Hardships often allow you to become more focused in your prayer times and to become specific with your requests. Difficulties can draw you toward God where the Refiner's fire can purify both you and your vision. God is never out to hurt or destroy us, but He is dedicated to perfecting us. God has often led me to self-examination for sin in my life or sin within my organization. And as uncomfortable as it may be, conflict forces us to ask those difficult questions. Confessing and repenting, even if it involves unintentional mistakes, can release the means for a turn-around!

Conflict Forces Us to Ask the Hard Questions

In spite of numerous victories, conflict surrounded us. We were losing money each year in the operational costs of our girls' programs in Deland and our Runaway Center in Daytona. During one year, we lost $65,000 in operations for the two centers combined. At our Bonifay Center, we were losing $25,000 annually, and we were pressed with building costs and the need for additional staff which, of course, meant additional salaries. We also needed new vans, and our insurance cost had doubled due to a recent hurricane within the area. Seeing how all these conflicts could possibly work to our advantage was a challenge in itself!

On a good note, our Ministry Institute was outgrowing its available space in Sanford, and we knew relocation was inevitable. We immediately began praying. As we discussed options, we felt our Daytona Beach property was the best site due to available space and the fact that the school would help us better utilize the building and consolidate some cost. When we submitted initial drawings for remodeling and presented them to the city, we ran into a snag. One member of the planning and zoning office suggested we not consider the move. He further explained that the city had future plans for a new parking garage and a water theme park in that area and the city might take our property by imminent domain. He was right. Within eighteen months, Daytona took our property.

However, this conflict blessed us. God took this challenge and turned it around for our good. In fact, the transaction proceeds we received were beyond our expectation. Daytona Beach paid us $585,000 for the building that originally cost us $290,000. We paid the balance of the note which was $175,000 and used the profit for debt reduction on our other facilities. We paid off our Sanford facility, our Davie Women's Home, and our Ft. Myers and Bonifay properties. Virtually all Teen Challenge debt was met with additional funding to invest in staff salaries. And if this were not enough, the Community United Methodist Church, located only a few blocks from us, offered the third story of their education building at no cost! As an added blessing, this church was positioned only one block from Main Street, a key street for runaways, bikers and kids at risk. God provided! God blessed and God expanded our possibilities!

At the church, we added our after-school at-risk program. The educational floor was just what we needed for classes and after school programs. We watched as God came through with space and several donated computers. We witnessed the growth of our ministry but more; we witnessed the impact on lives. One day while visiting our at-risk program, I met Karen.

Karen, an energy-packed eight-year-old, burst through the door excited to share with Bill (one of our staff) how her day at school had gone. She raced in, sat down at one of the computers and shared her daily account. Little Karen's mom is a lesbian who prostitutes herself and sells drugs for a living. Recently, she had brought a new lover into the home, one whom Karen could not stand.

Karen's mom is very arrogant about her lesbian choices and doesn't care what others think, especially Karen. Frequently, Karen cries when she speaks of her mother's friend. My heart breaks for Karen. This little girl is so sweet, and she has so much love to give. My prayer is for Karen's mother to be saved and for us to have enough time with Karen to make a difference in her life by teaching her some of Christ's redeeming and lasting truths.

Many nights have been spent in prayer for answers to Karen's needs and for others experiencing similar needs. Our staff labors diligently to reach those whom God brings into our care. Our ministry places great demands on our staff. Long hours, long nights, and many critical situations are typical of an average night. But with the grace of God, we have the joy of seeing lasting results. With a documented eighty-six percent cure rate, we often witness wonderful miracles in the lives of those who so desperately depend on us.

The miracle of changed lives is in itself addictive. Many workers who leave the Teen Challenge Ministry find themselves wanting to come back and often do. To be a part of the redemption of a young person who has been abused and beaten down by life is one of the most fulfilling experiences that you can encounter. Giving hope to the hopeless and help to the helpless is the ministry of Teen Challenge. This is what keeps us going. This is what keeps us going in the midst of great conflict.

With so many of our conflicts and challenges resolved, we needed to rethink our plans for housing the Ministry Institute. Again, we went to prayer for its relocation. Jacksonville was targeted as a possible site based on the number of churches in the area which supported us and based on the overwhelming number of calls we were receiving wanting to place students from that area. Because of the need, we began the search for property. Our endeavors led us to damaged hospitals, vacated apartment complexes, run down day care centers and finally 3333 Phillips Highway. The Plaza Motor Lodge, condemned for its condition, closed and vacant at that time was being used by transients as a place to live. As I walked through the motel going from room to room, I came across the remains of drug and alcohol abuse and prostitution. The life styles of its former residents were evident as I examined the remains of addictions and dependencies. Make shift crack pipes, designed from perforated soda cans, pornographic literature, and other remnants of destructive behaviors from the lost and hopeless haunted the rooms. Perhaps this was where we needed to be. Perhaps this was God's direction.

The property, one time listed at $400,000 had been reduced to $300,000. We offered $140,000 and a tax write off for the remainder. Praise God, the owners agreed; we signed the contract. We now had ninety days to research the zoning and make application with the city to allow Ministry Institute to reside at that location. Processes of zoning, inspections and public hearings lasted the full ninety days and then some, and these days were not without more conflict. During the zoning process, a local business owner decided he didn't want us near his store so he hired an attorney and went to battle against our zoning request. Conflict. Prayer. I couldn't believe it. Here we were doing God's will and someone wanted to hurt us and stop us from moving forward. Using this process to purify our vision and keep us on our knees, we then acted upon what I suspected God was directing us to do. We hired a well-respected Christian attorney who specialized in zoning issues and had built relationships with many on the zoning board. We allowed God to work through our lawyer, and we received the necessary zoning for our Ministry Institute. Plans of man will never alter the plans of God. Conflict resolved!

So, when conflict arises and it will come, use it to your advantage. Seek God's wisdom and the advice of Godly men. A miracle is in the midst of the chaos and God is most interested in how you decide to resolve the conflict. Remember, "All things work together for the good of them who love God and are called according to His purpose" (Romans 8:28). You are called. You will experience conflict. And you will experience the victory!

Principle 16:

SHARE YOUR BLESSINGS
WITH OTHERS

First Timothy 6:18 reads, "…be generous and willing to share. In this way, [you] will lay up treasures for yourself." The principle of reciprocity is a basic of God's nature. We've all heard, "You can't out give God." And we can't. Several years ago, He taught me His basic banking plan.

One day, while working with David Wilkerson, Brother Dave, during casual conversation with our staff, asked to borrow a twenty-dollar bill. Happy to assist, I pulled out the twenty and handed it to him. Brother Dave went on to explain, "When someone gives you something in one hand, place it in the other hand and pass it on. If you take it to your chest, secure it with the other hand and keep it all for yourself, then you don't have a hand free to receive more." He went on to point out, "Give what is given to you and God will keep giving to you in order that you can keep giving. You can't out give God, thus you will end up with all you need and then some!"

God proved His giving principle time and again and provided for our Jacksonville project in a most unusual way. During this time, I experienced that God is not provision limited. In fact, He has such an imagination and storehouse of means that He can far exceed what our minds can calculate. Let me illustrate.

I was invited to attend a district ministers' meeting where a pastor had challenged all the district churches to give sacrificially to a mission project in Bosnia. Knowing Teen Challenge's participation in the mission field and our executive board's decision to support many of our Teen Challenge leaders in foreign countries, I felt my obligations to our own ministry, and at first was not "moved" to contribute to the Bosnia cause. Nonetheless, my thinking was soon altered when God moved me.

While I sat in the service listening to this pastor from Bosnia, I became overwhelmed with the sensation that God wanted me involved. At first, I asked God if He were directing me to open a center in his area, but the Lord clearly indicated, "No, just help by giving." I was actually relieved that I didn't have to feel obligated to start another project and one in a foreign country at that; but still, funding a ministry when our own lacked was disturbing. Nevertheless, I continued seeking God's guidance on how we were to become involved, and I believed I heard His direction to give $5,000. Thinking to myself, "We don't have $5,000 to donate, and we've started building projects which require a minimum of $500,000," I sought advice. I leaned over to Wayne Gray, our Sanford facility director, and shared that I felt prompted to support this pastor's request. He agreed. We discussed figures, and I obeyed the Lord's promptings and pledged $5,000 through $1,000 monthly offerings over the next five months. Hear from God. Make plans by seeking wise counsel. Give unto others!

God was quick to respond. The next Monday, I received a call from a current donor who shared, "Jerry, my mom wants to contribute some money to Teen Challenge. She was going to set up a trust, but I suggested that she just go on and give you the donation now." I shared with this patron our obligations to current building projects and what a blessing it would be to have the money at that time. She contributed $50,000 in stock with a promise of an additional $50,000 at the first of the next year. Prayer was answered. Conflict resolved. And we had received abundantly more than we had even hoped for.

We used the first $50,000 toward the purchase of the Plaza Motor Lodge (the former haven of addictions, soon to be our future home for redemption) and combined with money from several supporters, we were able to purchase the entire property debt free. Our next challenge was to raise $175,000 for facility renovations and improvements for the parking area and exterior fencing. And even though those funds were the more difficult to raise, churches set up programs in which individuals could sponsor rooms for $5,000 each. We now have accommodations for 38 students in training for Teen Challenge staff positions and have just completed a $1,200,000 Student Life Center that houses a commercial kitchen, classrooms, offices and a lounge!

Through our fundraising encounters and support of other ministries and nonprofits, we built numerous lasting relationships. I am convinced that it is not a lack of money but rather a lack of relationships that can impede fundraising efforts. Build relationships with those in the community who are respected and influential and with those who share your same passions. Make new friends and nurture the commitments to old. Many of our graduates are now on staff, and many others support us faithfully through contributions and service.

One day, one of our students from the Sanford Center was with me when I stopped by our newly purchased Plaza Motor Lodge. He shared his story about how he had once lived in Jacksonville and had developed serious addiction to crack cocaine. He explained how he would come to the motel, meet up with other junkies, purchase his drugs and participate in all types of unacceptable behaviors. He shared that the results were horrible. His eyes, filled with remorse, slowly scaled the former motel, and then I watched as the eyes altered to a glisten. A simple smile widened his lips. He said, "Boy, it's good to see this place now used for the glory of God!" Thank God for His grace! He can change the life of a junkie! He can renew condemned motels. And He can fund it without a worry for provision. He is the Provision!

The principle of giving is a two-way street — giving and receiving. "Give and it shall be given unto you," the scriptures tell us. I learned this way of thinking at a very early age. I was six years old when my parents began giving me an allowance and taught me the value of giving, tithing and saving. From my weekly fifteen cents, five cents went into my giving jar, five cents into my savings and five cents into my pocket. Every allowance day, I would line up the jars and place the nickels into their proper places. I vividly remember taking my tithe to church and I vividly remember the savings jar becoming fuller and fuller. And I also remember running as fast as I could to the corner store to buy gum with the nickel in my pocket. At six, I had learned valuable truths. I gave God what was rightfully His, wisely saved for future investments and was blessed with Juicy Fruit at the same time.

Now, we have given thousands of dollars to various mission projects; we support college campus pastors and have assisted Teen Challenge directors from around the world to raise money. In one instance, our director from the Czech Republic came and within a period of two weeks had cash and pledges for $40,000. Teen Challenge in the Czech Republic was able to purchase a former museum where statues of Stalin and Lenin had once stood. That museum now serves as a church and a home for a women's center.

After the women's center had been established in Prague, Czech Republic, Petr Ministr, the director, came to me for some advice. We were in a Global Teen Challenge board meeting in Lithuania. Petr mentioned that in America the larger Teen Challenge centers have several induction centers and one large training center. I said, "Yes, that is the most utilized system."

He said, "I found a property that would allow us to expand our ministries as well as have space to open a church, several micro enterprises, and house over one hundred students. Do you think we should attempt to buy this to serve as our training center?"

As Petr was speaking to me I felt the Lord say to me, "I want you to partner with Petr on this project, in fact I want you to buy this building for their ministry."

As Petr described the facility I just listened and then told him, "Yes, this is a good move"— and that we would help him buy the property. I then asked him how much. Petr said $75,000. I asked how much time we had to get it to him. He said we would have six months. I felt we could do that, only to get a phone call a month later saying they had to have the money in thirty days and that the euro had risen and it would now cost $95,000 dollars.

I went to prayer and God gave me a plan. God spoke to me to ask each of our centers to raise $5,000 each, and I was to raise the rest. Each of the directors of the programs willingly stepped up to the challenge. In short, we sent $95,000 to the Czech Republic for the purchase of the facility. Since that time we have sent thousands more and several work teams to assist in remodeling their new training center. You cannot out give God. We have been blessed in untold ways since that time.

Not long after we gave that money, I received a call from a man who said he had been out looking for property when God spoke to him to look at the church property that was for sale next to the land he was looking at. He was confused: "Why would I want to look at church property?" But being faithful to the Lord, he did, and found that the church had 26,000 square feet of space, 43 acres of land, a commercial kitchen and six bathrooms with two showers in each bathroom. The Lord spoke to him to buy this property in Meansville, Georgia, for Teen Challenge.

He called me, told me the story and asked, "Jerry if I buy this and give this to you, will you open a Teen Challenge in it?"

I said, "Yes, you buy it and give it and I will be happy to open a boys home there."

One year later, the property appraised for one million six hundred thousand dollars, and we have a boys home there today. Praise God, you can't out give Him.

I had learned at an early age to give. The journey to adulthood can often haze the truths we know and understand. Doubt, fear and stress, the enemy's great tools, can overtake the childhood faith God so treasures. But God's faithfulness never wanes and He returns to us the financial principles of our youth, or teaches us these principles through His faithfulness of provision. Live out the indisputable economic laws of God:

1. We can't out give God!
2. And it's people, God's people, and not projects that meet our financial need.

The incorporation of these simple truths can lead to the abundance that can readily bless and allow your ministry to grow. Give it, then get it! Get it, then give it! When God blesses you with money, gifts or manpower, share it and wait. More blessing, more provision is on its way.

Principle 17:

GOD HAS PROVISION IN
UNEXPECTED OPPORTUNITIES

"Would you guys be interested in buying a car wash?" The question caught me by surprise and certainly opened an area unlikely for my consideration. "What in the world would we do with a car wash?" I remember thinking. Soap suds, broken change machines, clogged up vacs and spot free rinse did not need to be added to my agenda. We had undertaken several new projects and buying a car wash was not on my "to do" list at the time, and anyway we needed money for our own projects. A car wash? How ridiculous! How God!

My travel throughout the world has allowed me the privilege of understanding one fundamental Biblical truth, God owns it all! "The earth is the Lord's and everything in it . . . the world, and all who live in it" (Psalm 24:1). And in turn, 1 Timothy 6:17 explains that God provides us with everything. Therefore, God owns it all and God provides for His own. However, my world travels and experiences also taught me that God often uses the unexplainable and the unexpected to fulfill need and secure blessings.

So, we were asked, "Would you guys like to buy a car wash?" The owner of a full service car wash approached us with every intention of selling his state-of-the-art business. Although, he had invested several hundred thousand dollars to ensure a top quality facility, he was tired of running it and wanted to sell. And he wanted us to buy. And the reason he selected us was because of his admiration for one of our students. After hiring one of our Teen Challenge graduates, he was impressed with both his attitude and work ethic. Our graduate witnessed to co-workers and performed his duties with pride and integrity.

The owner, so impressed with this young man, wanted to hire more Teen Challenge students; yet, at the same time, decided to sell. The owner, a Christian, explained while in a prayer meeting, he felt the Lord speaking when the group was singing "We are Standing on Holy Ground." He felt the Lord impress that the car wash was holy ground. As he continued to pray, again he experienced the Lord's direction and came to us. I remember my bewilderment when Wayne Gray came to me saying a man named Mark Whitehead wanted to know if we'd like to buy his car wash. And unsure of what I was doing, we set up an appointment with Mark to discuss our possibility of being the next proud car wash owners!

Mark shared the story of God's presence during the prayer meeting. So, I listened carefully to his proposal. After looking at the numbers and taking a tour, it was evident that we needed to prayerfully consider the offer. The car wash was spotless, equipped with the latest technology. The lobby was ornate, the landscaping precise and even the bathrooms were meticulously decorated. We evaluated the cost, the revenue structure, the risks and the possible profit. Then we prayed. Most of all, we prayed.

And then, we got our answer. God wanted us to buy this business. And we did. And it blessed us. We have trained hundreds in the operation of this type of business and have exposed thousands of others to Teen Challenge. Handsome profits have rolled in each year, thereby, not only servicing the debt but also adding profits to our operations budget.

Owning a car wash was never in our fundraising plan. In fact, it was so far outside the box that we never spotted it. Innovative leadership is essential to funding your ministry. First, look for new opportunity. It may be a car wash, funnel cakes, or a skeet shoot. But God often uses the unexpected opportunity to provide need and future blessing. If He can use five loaves and two fishes, He can use a car wash! If He can place a gold coin in the mouth of a fish, He can use a car wash. Get away from the familiar and look for your car wash.

Secondly, utilize funding ideas you learn from others. While traveling the country, I glean ideas from other organizations and consider the tools that might work in our system. Developing and maintaining an open mind and a willingness to listen and learn from other ministries and businesses purposes larger possibilities for growth and securities.

Thirdly, innovative leaders take risks. Risks are a must when developing operating budgets for new start-up ministries and small businesses. Risks are taken upon God-direction and are covered in prayer. Many in leadership positions have no experience in taking risks. They pray, sit back, and want God to bring every provision to them. I have never seen this work. Those who are willing to climb out on the limb will discover the tools, locate the jobs and formulate the ideas that will enable survival and support for their mission.

Finally, innovative leaders disband fear. Fear cripples creativity. First John 4:18 states, "The one who fears is not made perfect in love," and verses repeatedly warn us to "fear not." Learning to trust God is a growing process that matures as we experience God's resources and never ending provision. As we trust Him, His truth becomes clear; God owns it all and He provides for His own.

Principle 18:

GET INVOLVED IN MISSIONS

Over the years, my staff and I have benefited from unlimited possibilities on the mission field. As our Teen Challenge ministry began to grow and capitalize a measure of success, opportunities to serve others through the truths we had learned while establishing and operating our non-profit came readily. One of these truths was the under-standing that God's heart longs for the lost and that He expects us to preach His Word and reach out to those who do not know His plan for redemption. Gifting us with use-able abilities and talents, we were ready to preach, teach, and serve wherever God sent us.

When mission opportunities arise, let me encourage you to take a step of faith and go. Travel to an area for which you are burdened or to a land where you recognize genuine need. When you give out of your ministry to aid the less-fortunate, those devastated from destruction, those in lack, or those perishing from the absence of the Lord's presence, God will in turn bless your ministry. We at Teen Challenge are amazed at the miracles we have been able to share with others.

People are drawn to those who do outstanding jobs. Remember God's law of giving, "When you get it, give it." So we began to share our knowledge with others. Estab-lishing a ministry from scratch requires a wellspring of information and trial/error applications that aid in filtering through what works and what doesn't. We should share both.

In 1992, leaders around the U.S. began calling us wanting to learn how to open and run a Teen Challenge center. When they called, I invited them to visit our Florida facilities and witness first-hand what we were doing and how we were doing it. And even though I didn't consider our accomplishments or operational means superior to what other leaders were achieving in this field, nor did I believe we had reached the level of success that warranted such attention, I was open to speak with others both locally and internationally about what God had taught us. My staff and I conveyed founding principles, mission statements, fundraising up's and down's, staffing requirements, operational costs, and personal success stories from many of our graduates. I answered their questions and then some. I shared within my area of expertise what I considered would benefit their programs.

In 1994, I attended the Twenty-fifth Anniversary Celebration of Teen Challenge Eurasia in Brussels, Belgium. During that conference, those attending decided that we needed to develop an International Fellowship to coordinate fellowship opportunities around the world as well as assist in the opening of Teen Challenge centers around the world. The International Fellowship was developed, and Don Wilkerson was asked (and agreed) to serve as the executive director. Immediately, founding members assisted Don in organizing a network of leaders from around the world. Calls came from India, Russia, South Africa, Albania, and countless additional countries requesting the opening of a center in their area. Locating the right workers, training and placing them, and funding new programs are overwhelming tasks; and we watched miracle after miracle as centers opened all over the world.

Earlier in 1993, I had led a team of our Ministry Institute students to Jamaica for a special missions project; and during the Twenty-fifth Anniversary Celebration in Brussels, a group of missionaries approached us about starting a center in Kingston. We left the conference with a burden to open this center as soon as God provided the personnel and the finances. Because of my interest in the Jamaican area, I was asked to serve as the Caribbean representative to the Board of Teen Challenge International Fellowship; and one day, I received a call from John Steigerwald requesting that we initiate a center in Jamaica.

Curiously, I asked, "Why are you interested in a facility in Jamaica, John?"

John responded that for years he had been involved in several mission trips to the area and had just experienced a very sad encounter. John had been witnessing in Montego Bay and ran across a lady in the streets who was apparently addicted to drugs. He wanted to get her some help and when he inquired where he could send her, the workers in the area told him that there was no Christian home for drug addicts. During that time, John said the Lord spoke to him about getting in touch with Teen Challenge and asking if they would start a center in Jamaica. He called me and shared the story, and I simply asked him if God were speaking to him to go and start this work. John began to pray and met with both Don Wilkerson and me to discuss the need and possibilities.

John did decide to go. He left the church he had started in Georgia, raised his support and moved his wife and four children to Kingston, Jamaica. The center is now open for men, and they are planning to open one for women.

International Relationships

Serving on the Global Teen Challenge Board has opened many opportunities for ministry throughout the world. Through the Board, I met Malcolm Smith from Perth, Western Australia, who invited me to come to Australia to train and share some of the fundraising ideas we were using in Florida. I couldn't believe it; someone was going to pay for me to travel halfway around the world to talk with them about what we were doing on the other side of the globe.

Malcolm got his money's worth. He worked me day and night. I taught a Turning Point seminar in one of the local churches, spoke at the grand opening of their new men's dorm, preached at several churches, and met with all of his board members and committees. Over dinner one evening, I shared with one board member our success with our golf marathon for fundraising.

The next day, this member returned to the board meeting claiming that his boss had agreed to donate $10,000 to help sponsor the event. During that first year, from one golf marathon, they raised $115,000. Needless to say, Malcolm Smith holds this event annually, resulting in similar profits. They have continued using the golf marathon event and have now raised over a million dollars to expand their ministry.

In the last years, residents from England, Germany, Canada, Dominica, Jamaica, Trinidad, Bahamas, Czech Republic, Portugal, Iceland, and numerous other nations have visited our Florida facility. In fact, some forty-five nations have scheduled our center for training and program observation. Some do internships and stay for several months while some are here for as little as a few days. Our desire is to serve anyone interested in Teen Challenge.

One particular group we felt honored to serve was the German Teen Challenge directors and secretary. Heinz called me from Germany wanting to spend a week and a half with us to evaluate our programs and utilize what they learned to make some significant changes in the structure of their current programs. They were also very interested in our organizational operation and in our fundraising tools. Since then, we, in turn, have toured all the Teen Challenge centers in Germany. They asked us to do a review of their programs and give them insight on how to go back to the roots and examine the basics on how Teen Challenge was developed. Serving our European neighbor allowed us to experience a different type of mission front, one in which we both were blessed.

I never cease to be amazed at the national and international affect this ministry is having on so many countries. Every story of the opening of a new center blesses me. Every visit to an international center heightens my expectations and my desire for growth. On my trip to Australia, I had a chance to stop by the Singapore Teen Challenge and meet Peter Misso. Peter gave me a tour of his facility, which was a former public school. Students of all ages were getting the needed help for their addictions, and it was a thrill for me to see how God was working in the lives of these students.

On another occasion, during one of our staff meetings, a gentleman interrupted without intention. He had made a wrong turn, and he apologized explaining that he had just come from Barbados to seek help for his son, an addict. He had heard that we had a great program and wanted the best recovery methods for Paul. Paul had become addicted to crack cocaine and had lost everything. He had hit bottom. His dad loved him enough to bring him to Florida for our help. God did just that. Paul was set free by the power of Christ and came to be one of the top graduates.

Paul graduated and decided to attend our Ministry Institute, which is a one year program designed to train staff for our centers. In the meantime, his dad began working on opening a center in Barbados and asked that we come and assist him.

A Vision Coming to Reality

Prior to my coming on as the executive director, Bob Manderscheid was serving as the president of the Teen Challenge Board of Directors. Having served on the board for more than twelve years, Bob had seen the good and the bad of Teen Challenge of Florida. At a time when the ministry was at an all-time low, considering closing the ministry down all together, with money problems and morality problems within leadership, God spoke to Bob and said, "One day people will come from all over the world to learn from Teen Challenge of Florida."

At that time, Bob had no idea how or when this would happen. He never told me about this special time with God until he heard me communicate stories about those coming for training. During a board meeting, Bob began to share what God had told him. His eyes teared up as he spoke of the vision God had given him for this work. Now, he was experiencing the fulfillment of that vision.

God has raised up great Teen Challenge centers throughout the United States. And I have had the honor to work with some of the most committed leaders of our facilities. Dennis Griffith from Southern California, Snow Peabody from Arizona, Mike Hodges from Oregon, Wayne Keylon from Tennessee, George Glover from Canada, Malcolm Smith from Australia, Tom Bremer and Joao Martins from Portugal, Petr Ministr from Prague, Czech Republic, and many others have all helped provide the tools that have added to our success. To quote George Glover, "An original idea is forgetting the source." We all work together and learn together and share ideas that will improve our centers and ministries. The opening of our *Rehoboth* was the evidence of hearing from God and following His direction. Teen Challenge of Florida has blessed many nations. Being a part of what God is doing around the world has been life changing!

What is important to learn is that as you get involved in missions, you will grow in ways you never imagined. You will expand your world view and your own ministry will be blessed as a result. As you give from your experience and as you give financially, you will be amazed how God returns those gifts one hundred fold. Your life is richer, your staff are blessed, and the students you take with you are exposed to ministry around the world. The benefits are worth the work and cost. Get involved in missions.

Principle 19:

GOD HAS A LEADERSHIP DEVELOPMENT PLAN DESIGNED FOR YOU

In 2 Chronicles 1:10, Solomon prays to God, "Give me wisdom and knowledge that I may lead this people...."

First, let me say that it is my conviction that effective leaders are not born but developed. No matter how you have come to where you are in your leadership responsibilities, God has divinely designed your life experiences to prepare you for your position. God utilizes your life experiences to prepare you, train you and tweak you. With wisdom, we listen to God's directives for our journey, stay prayed up and prepare for the venture. We armor up and implement His instructions while accepting His discipline and fine-tuning.

Secondly, in God's economy, He wants us to be where we are best suited and gifted. Learning to identify and operate within your gifts allows God to work His purpose through you. The day we find the perfect place where our gifts and our work line up with His will, we stop working. When you arrive "there," you know it! You won't feel like you're working, you simply will operate within the flow of your gifts and talents. You will feel as though you are "in your groove" and are being used for His intention.

Within our passions, we find unlimited energy, and we stop watching a time clock. Sound too good to be true? Well, it is not! If you are not currently working within the realm of your gifts, one day you will. You will realize that you are really enjoying what you do, how you do it, and how easy the job seems in spite of the conflicts. A God-led leader works within the scope of his talents and gifting.

By 2006, throughout the course of 15 years, we had opened twenty centers for boys, girls, men and women. With bed space for 1,054 students, we continue to press on and believe God to help us reach countless more who are desperate, hurting and hopeless.

A God-led leader sets goals and develops the plan to accomplish them. Teen Challenge is dedicated to transforming lives, one person at a time, and the more lives we impact tells us that we are being faithful to both God's blueprints and the provisions He has graciously placed in our paths. As God conducted us through His School of Life, we were able to open more centers and greatly expand our outreach. We traveled over bumps, came to dead ends and sometimes ran off the road. However, He used our past experiences to teach us, and thus, enabled us to become more effectual leaders. He has guided us to places I never dreamed possible.

The Dream Continues

The following centers I will mention are opened and filled with boys, girls, men, and women whose lives are being changed by God's power. We could have never dreamed of this kind of growth or this kind of success, but God has sent us some of the greatest staff and greatest donors who have made all this possible.

We have opened centers in Columbus, Georgia, where we bought a struggling golf and country club, and now have a one hundred bed girls' home. We bought a Methodist church and converted it into a fifty bed women's home which is now filled and running over with changing lives. We were given a property in Lakeland, Florida, worth a fortune which now houses forty girls. We bought an existing men's home in Vero Beach, Florida, and turned it into a forty bed boy's home. We merged with Mitch Melton and bought an elementary school in Dublin, Georgia, which now houses one hundred and fifteen men. The board of a struggling women's home ministry called and said they would give us their property in Jupiter, Florida, if we would run a female program there for three years. Today, the property is ours, and we have 22 girls in residence there. The property was worth over a million and a half dollars. We own it free and clear today.

What favor and what a joy to watch God bless this ministry with such wonderful properties. We have opened a men's home in Tallahassee, Florida, with the help of local donors there who fell in love with one of the graduates. They saw the dramatic change in his life and felt they needed a ministry like Teen Challenge in their city. In one luncheon I was handed $110,000 in cash and in another luncheon pledges of $300,000 more for developing this center. How God supplies when He touches the heart of someone. We have a men's home in Macon, Georgia, and are opening another one in Savannah, Georgia. We have a girls' home in Kansas City, Missouri, for forty and have other opportunities to expand in that region of the United States.

Only God knows how many centers we will develop beyond these twenty. Currently, we are expanding each of these to house more students. But to date, we have invitations to open additional centers in several major cities. If and when God gives the go-ahead, we'll set our focus to expand. Recently, I have had a special burden for the Miami and Tampa areas, and I am trusting God for property in those cities for Teen Challenge crisis centers. We are working on projects in several other cities. In the meantime, we will stay committed to God and await His next move.

After reading Bruce Wilkinson's *The Prayer of Jabez*, I felt challenged to pray as Jabez did. I prayed for God to bless me and expand my territory. I prayed that His hand would be with me and that He would keep me from evil. A God-led leader prays. With this prayer as a daily part of my life, as well as praying for favor with God and man, everyday, I expect God to continue to use me and the ministry of Teen Challenge.

A God-led leader expects miracles. For years, we have been able to count on those contributors who give ten- and fifteen-dollar monthly support as faithfully as we can our $500,000 donors. Every supporter is a valuable minister to our cause, and we respect all equally. Each doing what he can makes a difference in our world. And miraculously, the money always comes in. Money, property, equipment, appliances, curtains, dishcloths, and Christmas gifts – we always have enough!

Dennis Griffith, our southern California director claims, "We spend a dollar and a dime for every dollar we raise." And at times, it seems we do! Every dollar we raise is invested by providing more beds. Currently, our greatest challenge is to provide scholarships for our centers so we will always be able to provide beds for the hurting and can continue to run regardless of the state of the economy. We are encouraging donors to help build a scholarship fund at each location by giving generous gifts now and by including us in their wills or estates. A God-led leader plans for the future!

The previous projects took fifteen years to complete. Without solid leadership, Teen Challenge would not be the operational mission it now is. I became the leader God called me to be, but not without bruising, not without sacrifice and not without mistake. The journey I have so enjoyed has not been traveled on a freshly paved highway but rather on a rock-scattered dusty road. Each time I stumped my toe, I learned what worked and what didn't. But one of the greatest lessons I have come to understand is the realization that I could not do it alone. I need travel companions. A God-led leader chooses others who share the vision and are ready to act within their gifts. Choosing the right board of directors and the right staff is essential. The formation of a specialized team brings a wealth of creative possibilities to the worktable.

A God-led leader encourages commitment. God often has me reflect upon the prayer time in Winter Haven, upon the men, women, boys, and girls we work with. They are the reason we work so hard, the reason we punch through adversity. We are fortunate to work with staff who genuinely care for the students. Our staff, desiring God's best in our students' lives, developed a Student Covenant. It states, "We pledge to serve every student with Christ-like compassion, respect and guidance. We commit to address the needs of students and assist them in the development of Godly character. We dedicate ourselves to mentor and to nurture meaningful relationships, inspiring hope for the future." I believe every person who comes to Teen Challenge will experience this covenant because of the commitments of our dedicated staff. This commitment holds us accountable first to God, then to our students and to each other. At Teen Challenge, we reproduce men and women who have been God-led and in turn are ready to God-lead others!

Remember, God has a leadership plan for you. His plan is designed for you, and He will bless you with the wisdom and knowledge you need to develop it. Keep the following guidelines up front as you follow His directives to develop leadership within your ministry.

- God-led leaders work within the scope of their talents and gifts.
- God-led leaders set goals and develop the plans to accomplish them.
- God-led leaders pray.
- God-led leaders expect miracles.
- God-led leaders plan for the future.
- God-led leaders encourage commitment.
- God-led leaders surround themselves with those who support their vision.

God will send the right people your way. It's up to you to train, teach, and incorporate their talents and abilities into those areas where they can be best used and celebrated. God has a leadership development plan for you!

Principle 20:

KEEP CLOSE TO THE NEED

Staying focused on both the need and the people around you who are meeting that need are essentials to your ministry's growth. Remember, many times, the need is the call, and you must stay directed as to why you are doing what you do. As the need changes, refocus your efforts to reach its requirements. Secondly, you should carefully guard your heart to stay in tune with the need. The challenges of ministry, especially in the formative stages, are time consuming and stress-packed; you must avoid insensitivity in order to stay close to the need and to keep yourself available to be used by God.

Your nonprofit organization operates through the people you resource and often nonprofits must incorporate the assistance of willing volunteers. Frequently, these volunteers are experiencing or have experienced the same difficulties as those participating in your programs. Never give up on those God brings into your path. View them as an opportunity to value the joys and pain of working with uniquely troubled people, and remember that sometimes, these very tough ones are the very ones who get saved and are radically changed.

Knowing that God never sees any one of us as unreachable, when our Teen Challenge Choir holds church services, I almost always give an opportunity for those who have loved ones addicted to drugs or alcohol to come to the altar for prayer. The response is usually overwhelming and always heart touching.

Once, we were invited to minister at Suncoast Cathedral, a rather large church in St. Petersburg, Florida. About one hundred people came down for prayer that evening. Then, I invited others to come and join in prayer with those already at the altar. As I began the corporate prayer, a tugging on my coat suddenly distracted me. I looked down, continuing in prayer, to see a young boy still holding my jacket, looking up at me. He was probably around six, no more than seven years of age and had a desperate look in his eyes. I bent down and asked, "What do you need?"

"Mister, will you pray for my daddy?"

Kneeling down to his level, I put my arm around him and said, "Sure, son, I'll pray for your daddy; how can I pray for him?"

He looked up at me and answered, "He's on drugs." I then asked if his father lived at home, and he shared that his father was gone. So, I began to pray for this boy's dad and I asked God to free his dad from the drugs and bring his daddy home. My heart grieves for that young boy and every kid like him who just wants his daddy or mommy to come home.

Kids don't understand why their parents use drugs. Neither do they understand why their mommy or daddy would choose drugs over them. Often times they feel personally responsible for their parent's behavior. They often deduct that if they acted better, or were easier to care for or made higher grades, that their parent might respond to them differently. These children live with guilt and are constantly trying to change their behaviors in hopes that what they do will make a change. These children become laden with guilt when "everything" they try doesn't work. What a burden for a small child! As I stood praying with that little boy, I asked the church to join with us as we prayed again for this boy's daddy.

No one wakes up one morning claiming, "When I grow up I want to be a drug addict!" The desire to become drug dependent is not an inborn desire, but rather one that is developed through deep pain and lack of contentment in their lives. Drugs know no boundaries. Socioeconomic upbringings make no difference. Rich kids, poor kids? We have worked with the richest-of-the-rich and the poorest-of-the-poor and the bottom line is that people from all backgrounds and surroundings make bad choices.

Understanding our students' needs is innate to understanding their addictions and matching them with staff who can help them through the recovery period. Understanding is also crucial to building trust. As an organization striving to succeed and grow to reach more who are hurting, we understand that knowledge of the addiction progression is fundamental to what we do. Therefore, we choose qualified staff who train to do what they do and do it well. Whatever your organization is trying to achieve, whatever your purpose, you must thoroughly understand the steps in getting "there" and hand select those people who share your drive, your compassions and a willing spirit to learn.

The Addiction Process

Addiction is always a process. The first stage is the experimentation phase in which people begin to use drugs or alcohol socially—just a time or two a month, at parties or with friends. Generally, users begin with alcohol and progress to marijuana. Users soon learn that experimenting with the allurement makes one feel good, and then, they learn how to use the substance to make them feel great.

The second phase is the social stage in which the use is usually a weekly expectation. Not recognizing any serious or negative consequences, the user begins to trust the allurement and learns how to utilize the substance to his/her maximum advantage. They use during what they believe are appropriate times, and they make "safe rules" for themselves, believing that if they stay within the boundaries of the rules, they will be okay. They begin to lock in on trusting the compulsive behavior.

Eventually, the drug and/or alcohol use turns into a problem without warning, and the former "rules" are not providing the needed sensations. Progression to harder drugs, such as meth and crack cocaine, open the door for preoccupation. Preoccupation leads to daily use and harmful dependencies. The drugs now become an inherent part of what allows them to function in life. Their dependence has now reached harmful levels, and the user has lost control over their drug use.

Their value system is violated; they cannot block the emotional pain; while at the same time, their lifestyles center around their addiction. Physical health, spiritual lives, and relationships begin to deteriorate. Using is necessary just to feel "normal" and the user often becomes paranoid trusting no one and imagining the unrealistic. With no dignity and most often the breaking away of family and friends, the user moves from place to place hoping to escape. There is little desire to live. Without the drug's assistance, no longer is the user able to maintain normal life functions.

Individuals who fall into this trap get to the place where they cannot help themselves. Getting a job is difficult and keeping one is next to unheard of. Getting the money to maintain their habits often comes from prostitution, theft, and other illegal means. Drugs have become their gods. They can't stop using!

We need to reach out to those experiencing the horrors of drug and alcohol abuse. Family and friends should never attempt to help an addict by bailing them out, giving them money or paying their bills. Enabling will not produce healing. But rather, research the centers and facilities that may offer recovery programs and take an active role in setting up the help the addict may need.

Pray and Pray Again

Bailing out the addict actually contributes to their problems and prolongs the treatment they desperately call for. The law of the harvest is that you reap what you sow. Drug and alcohol abusers need to reap the consequences of their choices and experience the pain of addiction. Reaping is a vital part of their healing process. My best advice to you on how to get your loved one back on the right track with God and free them from addictions, is to pray. Pray, pray, and pray again that God will help them come to the realization that they must seek help. Then, pray for the facility or program that specializes in the support they require.

Recently, one of our graduates from many years back, came into my office for a visit. He had taken a relapse to alcohol and it had cost him dearly. He lost several excellent jobs that had blessed him and his family. While sharing his story, he made a statement that has had profound impact on me and on many. I found it well worth remembering. Realizing what his return to alcohol had cost him, he said, "My talents and abilities got me jobs that my character didn't allow me to keep." What a truth! How many have smooth-talked their way into a good paying job only to allow their character to sabotage their ability to keep it.

Staying close to our need helps sharpen character traits. Working with those with substance abuse and other disabling types of behaviors can be exceptionally draining to the emotions and can require unlimited hours of one-on-one teaching and personal involvement. Character is key to leadership and if you plan to keep a job, your character must be intact. This is true for the Teen Challenge worker and is a principle we teach our students. We focus on their need for healing and acceptance, and we focus on their need for self-sufficiency. We focus on their need to develop and maintain admirable character. Respect is earned through intact character; and, it is that admirable character which separates those who endure and will become future leaders from those who don't. Stay focused on the need!

Principle 21:

STICK TO THE BASICS

Stick to the basics! How many times have we heard that phrase? Regardless of the field, regardless of the project, there is always a point in time in which we have to assure balance and make certain that we have stayed true to the fundamentals. The greatest mathematician at the beginning of his educational journey took Basic Math. He may have been three years old at the time, but he had to learn the basics — basic addition, subtraction, multiplication and division.

During the 1970's, a new English curriculum introduced what was believed to be an easier approach to learning grammar skills. Transformational Grammar! No longer would restless students have to diagram sentences; there was an easier way to learn the parts of speech! Nationwide this approach began to spread to junior and senior highs. Faculties were convinced that this technique would allow students to immediately recognize direct objects and even know how to identify the very challenging predicative nominatives. Within two years, curriculum-planning committees were concluding that the schools needed to shelf the transformational methods and return to the basics.

An architect builds the foundation. The future chef, before he creates his own delicacies, uses recipes. The rock climber learns the basics in order to protect himself. The corporate CEO develops the team approach with a pyramid for growth. Fundamentals, nuts and bolts, the basics!

The twenty-one principles discussed in this book were not learned from textbooks, but rather from experience. Experience taught us both what worked and what didn't. From these times, we developed our training programs for our staff and our recovery and self-sufficiency programs for our students. I trust that some of the lessons that I learned will save you the pain of learning them the old fashioned way by touching the stove. Study the principles. Grasp them! Employ them as you do what God has called you to do. And may your passion, your dreams become reality!

PRINCIPLE # 1:
The leader must hear from God.

PRINCIPLE # 2:
Pray hard—work hard—pray God blesses your work.

PRINCIPLE # 3:
Cherish and celebrate victories along the way.

PRINCIPLE # 4:
Pray for favor with God and man.

PRINCIPLE # 5:
Stay true to your mission.

PRINCIPLE # 6:
Plan your growth.

PRINCIPLE # 7:
The church doesn't owe you a living.

PRINCIPLE # 8:
Develop the leaders around you and they will lead.

PRINCIPLE # 9:
Learn to laugh.

PRINCIPLE #10:
Opposition is a part of the process.

PRINCIPLE #11:
Lean into God's promise.

PRINCIPLE #12:
You can fund your mission.

PRINCIPLE #13:
Keep your family in focus.

PRINCIPLE #14:
Expect God to expand your original vision.

PRINCIPLE #15:
Use conflict to your advantage.

PRINCIPLE #16:
Share your blessings with others.

PRINCIPLE #17:
God has provision in unexpected opportunities.

PRINCIPLE #18:
Get involved in missions.

PRINCIPLE #19:
God has a leadership development plan for you.

PRINCIPLE #20:
Keep close to the need.

PRINCIPLE #21:
Stick to the basics.

The Miracles and Dreams Continue. . .

About the Author

JERRY NANCE, PhD

Jerry Nance has served since 1991 as the President/CEO of Teen Challenge of Florida/Georgia. Under his leadership, Teen Challenge has grown to over 20 centers in four states, caring for more than one thousand boys, girls, men and women.

Beginning in 1991 with one rented facility in Winter Haven Florida, Teen Challenge has since grown to include 7 juvenile centers, 4 women's centers, 8 men's centers, a bilingual men's center, a crisis center, and an administrative office. In addition there seems to always be opportunities to develop new centers.

Jerry graduated from Southwestern University with a B.S. in Christian Ministry, and then completed his Masters Degree in Counseling from Barry University. He has completed his PhD in Leadership, Education, with a specialization in counseling at Barry University.

Jerry served for five years as Crusade Associate for David Wilkerson, the founder of Teen Challenge. Working with World Challenge, he was responsible for organizing crusades and for developing and directing multiple major inner-city outreaches to reach drug-addicted people. He served as the senior pastor and as an associate pastor in several churches working with youth, counseling and developing programs for married couples.

Jerry serves on the Board of Directors of Teen Challenge USA. In 2007 he was asked to serve as President of Global Teen Challenge, after serving 12 years on their Board of Directors. He is responsible for providing leadership in training and assisting in developing centers in various countries around the world.

His passion for this ministry is evident in his commitment to share what he and his team of leaders have developed with Teen Challenge leaders around the world. The team of directors and staff Jerry gives oversight to now numbers more than 250. They are innovators of new curriculum, prevention programs, staff training programs, juvenile program conferences, and more. The servant leadership model is a part of the corporate culture.

Jerry and his wife, Libby, have been married for more than 30 years. They have 3 children who are all serving in the ministry in some capacity and they have 4 grandchildren.

Additional copies of this book and other publications by Dr. Nance may be purchased by phoning 706-596-8731 or going to the web site at

www.teenchallenge.cc

The office address is
15 W. 10th Street
Columbus, Georgia 31901